Real Talk And Recovery

Workbook

Melissa McKinney,
LAAC,MS,MA

Author's Note

This program was brought to you by lived experiences, extensive education, observation, assessment of others, and self-assessment. The use of AI helped to summarize information in a way that's clear and easy to understand. AI supported my ability to process large amounts of material quickly, which helped me focus more on meaningful insights, thoughtful reflection, and quality care.

This workbook can be used in a group with a facilitator or as a guide for individuals who are already strong in their recovery but are looking for a way to gain some much-needed self-awareness. Knowing yourself helps build confidence. You start to see your strengths and areas for growth, which fosters a sense of progress and motivation. Also notable, recovery is both healing and discovery. It acknowledges the past while embracing growth, resilience, and new identity. For many, the process involves rebuilding relationships, reestablishing purpose, and reclaiming agency over one's life. By using the language of recovery in all areas of behavioral health, the focus shifts from deficit and dysfunction toward transformation, renewal, and self-connection.

This program takes fundamental areas of recovery—exploring core beliefs, understanding your triggers and patterns, developing emotional awareness and regulation, and clarifying values and life purpose—by providing psychoeducation in the hopes that the reader better understands their importance in recovery.

Why Is This Program Different

This program is different because I have walked the same road. I'm not just a professional—I am in recovery myself. That means every tool, every exercise, and every word comes from lived experience, not just theory. There's no fluff here, no overpromising, and no pretending that recovery is easy. What you'll find instead is a straightforward, honest, and deeply human approach to change—one grounded in self-awareness, personal growth, and accountability.

At its core, this program blends two powerful therapeutic models: the *Humanistic Approach and the Behavioral Approach*. From a humanistic perspective, we believe in your inherent worth and your potential to grow. No matter what's behind you, you still have the capacity to heal, change, and move forward. You are not broken—you are becoming. This approach emphasizes empathy, acceptance, and the understanding that transformation begins when you start to see yourself clearly and value your own life.

On the behavioral side, this program recognizes that much of what we struggle with—addiction, avoidance, impulsivity—is learned behavior. And if they were learned, they can be unlearned. That's where behavioral modification comes in. We focus on small, consistent changes through reflection, structure, and practice. We ask you to look back—not to punish yourself—but to understand your patterns, learn from them, and do better moving forward.

Self-awareness is the heartbeat of this program. Without it, nothing changes. With it, everything can. Through daily check-ins, exercises and worksheets, psychoeducation, and reflective questions, you will begin to see yourself with new eyes and take ownership of your choices. You won't be doing this alone, and you won't be doing it for anyone else. This is your work. Your life. Your path. And we're here to walk it with you.

Welcome to Your Real Talk and Recovery Journey

We're so glad you're here! By opening this workbook, you're stepping into a sacred space of healing, growth, and rediscovery. This journey is not about perfection—it's about progress, connection, and remembering who you truly are underneath the weight of survival. Whether you're just beginning or continuing your recovery path, know that you are not alone. You are seen. You are valued. You are *enough*.

Over the next *30* days, this workbook will guide you through four gentle but powerful pillars of transformation:

- Exploring Core Beliefs & Identity
- Understanding Your Triggers & Patterns
- Developing Emotional Awareness & Regulation
- Clarifying Values & Life Purpose

Each of these sections invites you to reflect, write, feel, and grow—with compassion and curiosity rather than judgment. Recovery is not linear, and healing rarely looks like a straight line. It's okay to have setbacks, pauses, or moments of resistance. That's part of the process. What matters most is that you keep showing up for *yourself*.

The Heart of the Journey

Exploring Core Beliefs & Identity

Have you ever paused to ask yourself: *Where did these beliefs about myself come from?* In this section, you'll begin peeling back the layers of conditioning, trauma, and expectation that may have shaped your view of yourself. You'll get to explore the difference between who you truly are and who you've been told to be. We'll hold space for your identity as more than labels—you're not your diagnosis, your mistakes, or your roles. You are a full, complex, and evolving human being. As you reconnect with your authentic self, you'll begin to notice the quiet but powerful truth that your worth has never been up for debate.

Understanding Your Triggers & Patterns

Here, we'll get curious about your emotional world—not to judge it, but to understand it. Triggers are not weaknesses—they're signals. They point to places inside of us that still need safety, care, or healing. This section helps you track your patterns, decode your responses, and gently connect the dots between your past experiences and present reactions. With awareness comes choice. And with choice comes freedom. It's not about "fixing" yourself; it's about learning to support and soothe yourself, moment by moment.

Developing Emotional Awareness & Regulation

We often hear "feel your feelings," but what does that actually mean? Emotional awareness is the practice of naming, noticing, and making room for what arises within you. It's learning that emotions are messengers—not enemies. In this part of the journey, you'll explore tools for self-regulation, grounding, and expression. You'll learn to ride the emotional waves without drowning, to offer yourself kindness during storms, and to understand that emotional strength is not about suppression—it's about integration.

Clarifying Values & Life Purpose

This is where your story turns toward the future. Once you understand who you are and what you need, you can begin to shape a life that feels meaningful and aligned. This section helps you identify your core values—those deep truths that guide your decisions, relationships, and goals. You'll start envisioning a life rooted in authenticity and purpose—not just surviving, but truly living. Not just reacting, but creating. Your life matters. Your voice matters. Your healing has a ripple effect.

You are not behind. You are not broken. You are becoming.

You may cry, laugh, rage, or feel numb during this journey. All of it is okay. All of it is welcome. Just remember—healing isn't something you do perfectly. It's something you live a little more fully each day. We are honored to walk beside you.

What Is This All About?!

Over the next four weeks, we'll explore key areas that are essential to early recovery. Each week focuses on a different theme, helping you build insight, develop new tools, and prepare for the challenges and victories ahead.

Getting Started: Creating a Therapeutic Space

Welcome to your healing space. Whether you're joining a group session or engaging in quiet reflection on your own, setting the scene is key to creating a safe, supportive environment for growth and recovery.

Here's how to get started:

Set the Tone with Lighting: Keep lights low and gentle. Soft lighting helps create a calm, non-intrusive atmosphere that invites reflection and emotional safety.

Incorporate Soft Sounds: Consider playing calming background music, nature sounds, or simple white noise. These sounds help ground the space and minimize distractions.

Maintain Consistency: Try to keep the setting consistent day to day. Familiarity fosters trust and emotional ease—both essential for therapeutic work.

Limit Traffic and Distractions: Choose a low-traffic area where interruptions are minimal. Physical privacy supports emotional openness.

Practice Mindfulness: Arrive with intention. Take a few breaths. Notice your thoughts, your body, and the energy of the space.

Be Open-Minded and Respectful: Whether you're alone or with others, bring a spirit of curiosity and non-judgment. Respect each person's process—including your own.

With or Without a Facilitator: Healing can happen in many forms. This space supports guided sessions or solo reflection. You are welcome either way.

Let this space remind you: you are safe, supported, and allowed to grow.

To work toward the overall goal of consistency, each week will be set up the same way. Each week will start with an introduction and objective, and some final thoughts at the end of the week. Also, within every week, each day will offer the following format:

- **Learning Opportunity**
- **Self-Assessment**
- **Worksheet**
- **Journal Prompts**
- **Activity**

As a bonus, there are some personal recovery stories of amazing people I have met sprinkled throughout the workbook.

As you move through the next 30 days, may this workbook be a space for honest reflection, self-discovery, and growth.

1

Exploring CORE beliefs & identity

Introduction

Exploring Core Beliefs & Identity begins by understanding the origins of our core beliefs—those deeply held ideas about ourselves, others, and the world that often form in childhood and are shaped by family, culture, religion, and life experiences. These beliefs can be empowering or limiting, often operating unconsciously to influence our behaviors, decisions, and self-worth. By identifying and challenging limiting beliefs, individuals can begin to reframe their internal dialogue, build self-compassion, and move toward a more authentic and empowered sense of self. This process of self-inquiry helps uncover the "why" behind our thoughts and behaviors, offering insight into how past experiences continue to shape present realities.

Values clarification is another key part of strengthening personal identity. When we clearly define what truly matters to us—independent of external expectations—we build a stronger foundation for decision-making and self-expression. This alignment allows us to live more authentically, which directly impacts our relationships. Core beliefs affect how we give and receive love, how we trust, and how we set boundaries. When these beliefs are rooted in shame or fear, they can lead to disconnection or codependency. However, by healing and reshaping those beliefs, individuals can cultivate healthier, more fulfilling connections based on mutual respect, vulnerability, and shared values.

Objective

The objective of this section is to guide individuals in exploring the origins and influence of their core beliefs in order to develop a clearer, more empowered sense of identity. Through examining where these beliefs come from, challenging those that are limiting, and clarifying personal values, participants will gain insight into how their beliefs shape their self-image, life choices, and relationships. This self-awareness fosters personal growth, emotional resilience, and the ability to form healthier, more authentic connections with others.

W1: Agenda

M	Origins of Core Beliefs & Identity
T	Challenging Limiting Beliefs
W	Values Clarification and Personal Identity
T	The Impact of Core Beliefs on Relationships
F	Shifting Identity Through Growth and Recovery
S	Mindful Movement & Nature Connection

Monday

Origin of Core Beliefs

Exploring Core Beliefs & Identity: The Origins of Core Beliefs

Our core beliefs are the deeply rooted ideas we hold about ourselves, others, and the world around us. These beliefs are often unconscious but serve as the lens through which we interpret experiences, form relationships, and make decisions. Exploring where these beliefs come from is an essential part of understanding our identity. It allows us to uncover patterns that have been guiding us for years—often without us realizing it. When we take the time to explore the origins of these beliefs, we begin the powerful process of reclaiming our personal narrative, shifting from outdated programming to intentional, self-empowered living.

Core beliefs usually begin forming in early childhood. During this stage of life, we absorb messages from caregivers, family dynamics, cultural norms, schooling, religious teachings, and social experiences. Because young children are not yet equipped to critically analyze or challenge information, they often internalize these early messages as absolute truths. For example, a child who is consistently praised for achievements but ignored when vulnerable may form a belief that they are only valuable when they are successful. Similarly, a child who is criticized or neglected may adopt a core belief that they are unworthy of love or inherently flawed. These beliefs don't remain static—they evolve and show up in our adult lives as thought patterns, emotional triggers, and relationship habits.

Understanding the origins of our core beliefs is important because it creates space between who we truly are and the messages we've internalized over time. Many limiting beliefs—such as "I'm not good enough," "People can't be trusted," or "I must always be in control"—are rooted in early experiences that are no longer relevant or accurate. Yet, if left unexamined, they continue to shape our sense of identity, often leading to anxiety, low self-esteem, perfectionism, or people-pleasing behaviors. **By identifying where a belief came from and why we adopted it, we gain the power to decide whether it still serves us.** This awareness becomes a tool for transformation, helping us choose thoughts and actions that reflect our current values rather than old wounds.

Exploring the roots of our beliefs also has a profound impact on our relationships. Core beliefs influence how we see ourselves in relation to others—whether we believe we are lovable, whether we trust easily, or how we respond to conflict. For instance, someone who holds the belief "I have to earn love" may find themselves in unbalanced or codependent relationships, always giving more than they receive. On the other hand, someone who believes "I will be abandoned" may push others away out of fear, reinforcing the very outcome they dread. These patterns can keep us stuck in cycles of disconnection, unless we become aware of the beliefs that drive them. By unpacking the origins of these beliefs, we can begin to relate to others from a place of self-worth and authenticity, rather than fear or defense.

Ultimately, **exploring the origins of core beliefs is not about blaming the past—it's about reclaiming agency over your present and future.** It's an invitation to pause, reflect, and ask: *Is this belief true? Where did it come from? Does it reflect who I am now, or who I was trying to survive as then?* When we engage in this work with compassion and curiosity, we make room for a more empowered sense of self to emerge—one that is built on clarity, intention, and alignment with our true values. In doing so, we reshape not only our inner world but also the way we show up in our relationships, communities, and life path.

Exploring the origins of your core beliefs can feel vulnerable at first, but it is one of the most transformative steps toward emotional freedom and self-actualization. As you identify what shaped you, you'll begin to see that your story doesn't end there. **You have the power to write new chapters—ones that are rooted in truth, strength, and your unique sense of purpose.** Through this work, you gain not just insight but the opportunity to live in alignment with your most authentic self.

Self-Assessment

Exploring Core Beliefs & Identity

Instructions: Answer each question honestly. Then, use the scale below to find your score.

1. I can identify specific messages I received in childhood that shaped how I view myself today.
2. I notice patterns in my thoughts or behaviors that seem to come from past experiences, even if they no longer serve me.
3. I often question whether the beliefs I hold about myself are still accurate or helpful.
4. I feel comfortable exploring uncomfortable or painful parts of my past in order to grow.
5. My core beliefs help me feel grounded, empowered, and aligned with who I truly am.
6. When I experience emotional triggers, I try to trace them back to their root causes.
7. I am aware of how my core beliefs affect my relationships, including how I communicate and set boundaries.
8. I believe I have the power to challenge and change limiting beliefs that no longer reflect who I am.

1 – Strongly Disagree	2 – Disagree	3 – Neutral /Unsure	4 – Agree	5 – Strongly Agree

Scoring Guide:

8–16:
You may be just beginning your journey of exploring your core beliefs. Start with curiosity and compassion—there is deep insight waiting beneath the surface.

17–28:
You are developing awareness of your inner narrative and how it was shaped. Keep reflecting, journaling, and exploring the connections between your past and present.

29–40:
You have a strong sense of self-awareness and are actively working to reshape your beliefs and identity. Continue nurturing this growth—it's helping you live with greater authenticity and freedom.

Worksheet: Where Did That Belief Come From?

Topic: *Exploring the Origins of Core Beliefs and Their Impact on Identity & Relationships*

Objective: To help you identify, examine, and challenge one core belief that has influenced how you see yourself and relate to others.

____

____

____

____

Step 1: Identify a Core Belief

Think about a belief you hold about yourself. It could sound like:

"I'm not good enough."

"I always mess things up."

"I have to take care of everyone."

"I can't trust people."

"Success defines my worth."

Write your core belief here:

____

____

____

____

Step 2: Explore the Origin

Now reflect on where that belief might have come from. Consider:

Childhood experiences

Family dynamics

Cultural or religious influences

School or peer experiences

Traumatic or repeated events

When do you remember first feeling this way or hearing this message?

____

____

____

____

Who or what influenced this belief the most?

____

____

____

____

What was going on in your life during that time?

____

____

____

____

Step 3: Examine the Impact

How has this belief affected your identity? (How do you see or treat yourself?)

____

____

____

____

How has this belief shown up in your relationships?

____

____

____

____

What emotions come up when you think about this belief?

____
____
____
____

Step 4: Reframe and Empower

Is this belief 100% true today? If not, what's a more balanced or empowering version of it?

Original belief: ____
New belief: ____

How would your life or relationships shift if you truly believed this new, empowering thought? Use the next page to reflect on this idea.

____
____
____
____
____
____
____
____
____
____
____
____
____
____
____
____
____
____
____
____

Journal

1. What messages did I hear about myself growing up?

2. What roles did I play in my family (e.g., caregiver, peacekeeper, rebel)?

3. Were there specific experiences that shaped how I view myself or others?

Activity

The Importance of Family & Belief Mapping

Mapping your family and belief systems helps uncover the roots of your values, behaviors, and emotional patterns. It reveals how generational influences, cultural norms, and early experiences have shaped your identity and worldview. By visually connecting these influences, you gain insight into what beliefs truly align with who you are today—and which ones may need to be challenged or released. This process can foster greater self-awareness, healing, and intentional growth.

HOW TO: Family & Belief Mapping

Draw a simple timeline from early childhood to now.

Along the line, write down key messages or lessons you received (e.g., “Don’t show weakness,” “Work = worth”).

Circle the beliefs that still influence you today.

YEAR	*KEY MESSAGES OR LESSONS YOU RECEIVED*

Courtney

Personal Recovery Story

Before I got sober, alcohol was my go-to coping mechanism. It began at 19 years old, socially, as it does for many, but over time, it evolved into something dark and very problematic. I went through spurts over ten years, where it was drinking every day, to moderation, to binge drinking. At first, it helped me come out of my shell, and then it numbed the stress, anxiety, and disappointments. But eventually, it stopped working, and the shame and chaos crept in. I was stuck in a cycle of regret, anxiety, and trying to "control" my drinking. It impacted every part of my life: my relationships, my mental health, my energy, and my ability to show up fully. I looked fine on the outside, but inside, I was exhausted and disconnected and slowly dying.

What worked for me was finding a path that allowed me to explore recovery in a way that honored who I was. I took a holistic and personalized approach that included everything from white-knuckling it to twelve steps to therapy to coaching to building a sober community, addressing my emotional health, and learning tools to feel and deal with life. I realized sobriety wasn't just about not drinking—it was about creating a life I didn't want to escape from.

Today, life is fuller, more fun, more authentic, and grounded in peace. I'm proud of the woman I've become: resilient, self-aware, and empowered. My relationships are stronger, I'm present in my life, and I've learned how to show up for myself and others in ways I never could before. I don't have to hide anymore. I've found purpose in helping other women take their first steps toward sobriety, too. My sober date is August 18, 2012, and it's a day I celebrate every year, not just for the choice I made, but for the freedom it brought into my life.

Courtney Andersen

Sober Coach, Podcast Host, Author, Founder of Sober Vibes and National Sober Day

@sober.vibes

www.courtneyrecovered.com

tuesday

Challenging Limiting Beliefs

Rewriting Your Inner Narrative

As we begin to explore our core beliefs and how they shape our identity, we often encounter ideas that no longer serve us—thoughts like *"I'm not good enough," "I can't trust anyone,"* or *"I'm destined to fail."* These are called limiting beliefs, and although they may have once served a protective or adaptive purpose, they can now keep us stuck in cycles of fear, shame, and disconnection. Challenging these beliefs is a key part of reclaiming your identity and stepping into your full potential. It allows you to break free from patterns rooted in old narratives and start living in alignment with your truth, values, and strengths.

Limiting beliefs often begin in childhood, formed through repeated experiences, family messaging, societal expectations, or painful moments that left emotional imprints. For example, if you were constantly compared to a sibling or only rewarded for being quiet and obedient, you might have developed the belief that your voice doesn't matter. Over time, these beliefs become so ingrained that they feel like facts, rather than interpretations of past events. **The danger lies in their invisibility—many people don't realize they're operating under the weight of a limiting belief until they start noticing patterns of self-sabotage, low confidence, or unfulfilled potential.** These beliefs may affect everything from career decisions and relationships to how you handle conflict or express emotions.

Challenging limiting beliefs doesn't mean simply "thinking positive" or ignoring reality. It's a process of compassionate self-inquiry and mental reconditioning. The first step is awareness—noticing the thoughts that arise in response to stress, failure, success, or vulnerability. When you hear an internal voice saying, *"I'll never be good at this"* or *"I don't deserve love,"* pause and question it. Ask yourself: *Where did this thought come from? Is it absolutely true? Would I say this to someone I care about?* By bringing these thoughts into conscious awareness, you create distance between your identity and the belief—you realize that *you are not your thoughts.*

Once you've identified a limiting belief, the next step is examination and reframing. This means looking at the evidence for and against the belief, and then constructing a more balanced, empowering perspective. Let's say you hold the belief *"I always fail."* Instead of accepting it as truth, look for counterexamples: times when you succeeded, grew, or showed resilience. From there, reframe the belief into something more accurate and compassionate, like: *"I have experienced failure, but I've also learned and grown from it."* **Reframing isn't about pretending everything is perfect—it's about building a belief system that honors your reality while also supporting your growth.**

The impact of challenging limiting beliefs goes far beyond just "feeling better." It reshapes how you see yourself, how you interact with others, and how you approach life's challenges. In relationships, for example, a limiting belief like *"I'm not worthy of love"* can lead to people-pleasing, fear of abandonment, or emotional withdrawal. When that belief is challenged and replaced with *"I am enough just as I am,"* you begin to set healthier boundaries, attract more balanced connections, and speak your truth without fear. Similarly, in your personal and professional life, releasing beliefs like *"I'm not capable"* opens doors to taking risks, expressing creativity, and pursuing goals with more confidence and intention.

Challenging limiting beliefs is a gradual process—it requires practice, patience, and support. These beliefs were often formed over years and are reinforced by habit and emotion, so they won't disappear overnight. **But with each limiting belief you bring into the light and challenge, you take back a piece of your power.** You start to live more from your truth and less from your fear. You stop operating on autopilot and begin consciously designing your life in alignment with who you truly are.

Ultimately, this work is about identity. Who do you believe you are? And who do you want to become? By challenging the old beliefs that no longer align with your values or potential, you make space for a more authentic, empowered version of yourself to emerge. **It's not about becoming someone new—it's about returning to who you've always been beneath the layers of doubt, fear, and conditioning.** You are not broken. You are becoming. And challenging your limiting beliefs is one of the most powerful ways to step fully into that becoming.

Self-Assessment

Challenging Limiting Beliefs

Instructions: Rate each statement on a scale from *1* (Strongly Disagree) to 5 (Strongly Agree).

1. I am aware of the negative or limiting beliefs I hold about myself.
2. When I notice a limiting belief, I try to understand where it originated.
3. I actively question whether my self-limiting beliefs are true or helpful.
4. I find it difficult to challenge negative thoughts or beliefs about myself.
5. I can reframe a limiting belief into a more positive or balanced thought.
6. Challenging my limiting beliefs has helped improve my relationships with others.
7. I feel empowered to replace old, limiting beliefs with new, healthier ones.
8. I believe that changing my core beliefs can positively impact my identity and life.

1 - Strongly Disagree	2 - Disagree	3 - Neutral /Unsure	4 - Agree	5 - Strongly Agree

Scoring Guide:

8–16:

You might be in the early stages of recognizing and challenging limiting beliefs. Consider starting with self-awareness exercises and gentle reflection.

17–28:

You are developing a growing awareness and are beginning to question and reframe limiting beliefs. Keep practicing and exploring.

29–40:

You are actively challenging limiting beliefs and creating empowering new narratives. This work is strengthening your sense of self and well-being.

Worksheet: Challenging Limiting Beliefs

Step 1: Identify a Limiting Belief

Write down one negative or limiting belief you often notice in yourself (e.g., "I'm not good enough," "I can't trust others," "I'm a failure").

Belief:

____

____

____

____

Step 2: Explore the Origin

Reflect on where this belief might have started. Consider your childhood, family messages, experiences, or cultural influences.

- When do you first remember feeling or hearing this belief?

  ____

  ____

  ____

  ____

- Who or what influenced this belief?

  ____

  ____

  ____

  ____

- What was happening in your life at that time?

  ____

  ____

  ____

  ____

Step 3: Examine the Impact

How has this belief affected:

- Your self-image and confidence?

- Your relationships or interactions with others?

- Your choices and actions in life?

Step 4: Challenge and Reframe

Ask yourself:

- Is this belief absolutely true?

- What evidence contradicts this belief?

- What is a more balanced, positive belief you can adopt?

____
____
____
____

- Write your new, empowering belief here:

____
____
____
____

Step 5: Imagine the Change

How would your life be different if you truly believed this new statement?

____
____
____
____
____
____
____
____
____
____
____
____
____
____
____
____
____

Journal

1. What negative things do I often say to myself (internally or out loud)?

2. When did I first start believing this?

3. How true is this belief today?

Activity

The Importance of Recognizing Your Beliefs as an Activity

Engaging in activities that help you identify and examine your core beliefs encourages self-reflection and personal growth. By actively exploring what you believe about yourself, others, and the world, you can begin to understand how these beliefs influence your choices, relationships, and emotions. This intentional process creates space to challenge limiting beliefs and replace them with more empowering, authentic ones that support your recovery and well-being.

HOW TO: Belief Challenge Worksheet:

Create a chart with the following columns:

- Limiting Belief
- Evidence for
- Evidence Against
- New Empowered Belief

Limiting Belief	Evidence for	Evidence Against	New Empowered Belief

Wednesday

Values Clarification and Personal Identity

Values Clarification and Personal Identity

Discovering What Truly Matters

Exploring core beliefs and identity is a profound journey of self-awareness and growth, and central to this process is the practice of values clarification. Values are the deeply held principles and standards that guide our decisions, behaviors, and sense of purpose. They act like an internal compass, helping us navigate life's challenges and opportunities with integrity and authenticity. **When we clarify our values, we gain greater insight into what truly matters to us—beyond external expectations, societal pressures, or inherited beliefs.** This clarity is essential to building a strong, grounded personal identity that reflects our unique truth and enables us to live with intention.

Values typically develop through a complex interplay of influences, including family, culture, education, and life experiences. However, as we mature and begin to explore our identity more consciously, it becomes vital to differentiate between values we have absorbed from others and values we have chosen for ourselves. This process of clarification invites us to question: *Which values resonate deeply with me? Which ones feel imposed or outdated?* **By distinguishing our authentic values, we can shed layers of conditioning that no longer fit and make room for a more empowered and coherent self.** This is especially important because unclear or conflicting values often lead to confusion, inner conflict, or feelings of being "lost" or "off track."

Clarifying values helps to illuminate the roots of our core beliefs by revealing the motivations behind our thoughts, feelings, and actions. For example, someone who values *authenticity* highly may recognize that a core belief like "I must please everyone" conflicts with their desire to be true to themselves. Conversely, if *security* is a primary value, beliefs that emphasize safety and control may feel more comfortable and natural. Understanding these connections deepens self-awareness, allowing us to better understand why certain beliefs took hold and how they influence our identity. It also offers a roadmap for change, showing where we might need to realign our beliefs to better support our values—and, consequently, our wellbeing.

The importance of values clarification extends beyond personal insight; it shapes how we relate to others and the world around us. **When we live according to values that feel authentic, we communicate more honestly and connect more meaningfully.** Our relationships become a reflection of our true selves, rather than a performance shaped by external demands. This alignment fosters greater self-respect and respect from others, creating healthier boundaries and deeper trust. Moreover, clear values help us navigate ethical dilemmas and life decisions with confidence, reducing anxiety and second-guessing. In essence, values act as the foundation upon which a stable, integrated identity is built.

However, clarifying values is not always straightforward. It often requires peeling back layers of cultural conditioning, family expectations, and even fears that have obscured our authentic priorities. This can bring discomfort or uncertainty as we question long-held beliefs and habits. But this discomfort is a sign of growth—like stretching a muscle to build strength. Tools such as reflective journaling, guided questioning, and values sorting exercises can support this process, helping us articulate what truly matters and why. Over time, this practice cultivates a deeper connection to our inner selves and a clearer sense of purpose.

Ultimately, values clarification is a dynamic and ongoing part of exploring core beliefs and identity. **As we evolve, so too can our values—and embracing this evolution allows us to continually refine who we are and how we want to show up in the world.** This journey empowers us to live deliberately, guided not by outdated beliefs or external pressures, but by our own heartfelt convictions. By understanding and honoring our values, we lay the groundwork for a fulfilling life marked by authenticity, integrity, and connection.

In summary, clarifying your values is a transformative step in the journey of exploring core beliefs and personal identity. It helps uncover the roots of your internal beliefs, aligns your choices with your true self, and strengthens your relationships and sense of purpose. Through this ongoing work, you gain the clarity and courage to live fully as who you are—beyond roles, expectations, and limiting beliefs—and to create a life that resonates deeply with your most authentic identity.

Self-Assessment

Value Clarification & Personal Identity

Instructions: Answer each question honestly. Then, use the scale below to find your score.

1. I have a clear understanding of what my most important personal values are.
2. I can identify values that I inherited from others, but no longer feel true to me.
3. I regularly reflect on whether my daily actions align with my core values.
4. When making decisions, my personal values guide my choices more than external pressures.
5. I feel confident expressing my values openly in my relationships.
6. I am aware of how my values influence my core beliefs about myself and others.
7. I feel a strong sense of personal identity based on the values I have chosen for myself.
8. I am open to revisiting and refining my values as I grow and change.

1 – Strongly Disagree	2 – Disagree	3 – Neutral /Unsure	4 – Agree	5 – Strongly Agree

Scoring Guide:

- **8–16:**

You may be beginning to explore your values. Consider spending more time reflecting on what truly matters to you.

- **17–28:**

You have some awareness of your values, but might benefit from deeper clarification and practice aligning with them.

- **29–40:**

You have a strong connection to your personal values and use them effectively to guide your identity and life choices.

Values Clarification & Personal Identity Worksheet

Step 1: Identify Your Core Values

List 5–10 values that resonate with you. These are principles or qualities that feel deeply important. Examples: honesty, compassion, creativity, independence, family, growth, and fairness.

1. ____________________
2. ____________________
3. ____________________
4. ____________________
5. ____________________
6. ____________________
7. ____________________
8. ____________________
9. ____________________
10. ____________________

Step 2: Reflect on Origins

For each value you listed above, briefly answer:

- Where did this value come from? (Family, culture, experience, etc.)
- Why is this value important to me?

Example:
Value: Honesty
Origin: My parents always emphasized telling the truth.
Importance: It builds trust and helps me feel authentic.

____
____
____
____

Step 3: Prioritize Your Values

Look over your list and choose your top 3 most important values. Write them here:

____

____

____

____

Step 4: Values in Action

For each top value, describe how you currently express it in your daily life.

Example:
Value: Compassion
In Action: I volunteer at a local shelter and listen carefully when friends need support.

____

____

____

____

Step 5: Values and Identity

Answer these questions to deepen your understanding of how your values shape your identity:

How do these values reflect who I am at my core?

Are there any values I feel pressured to hold that don't truly resonate with me?

How do my values influence my choices and relationships?

____

____

____

____

Step 6: Aligning with Your Values

Consider one area of your life (work, relationships, self-care, etc.) where you feel out of alignment with your values. What is one step you can take to bring this area more in line with what truly matters to you?

Journal

1. **What qualities do I admire in others?**

2. **What makes me feel proud or fulfilled?**

3. **When do I feel most "like myself"?**

Activity

The Importance of Taking a Core Value Inventory

Taking a core value inventory helps you clarify what truly matters to you at your deepest level. By identifying your guiding principles, you can make more aligned decisions, set meaningful goals, and live with greater purpose. This process also highlights any disconnect between your current actions and your values, offering an opportunity for realignment and personal integrity—especially important during recovery and life transitions.

HOW TO: Core Value Inventory

Choose your top 10 values (e.g., honesty, compassion, justice, freedom).

Narrow it down to your top 3.

Write a paragraph about how these values show up in your daily life and decisions.

Core Value Inventory

Some Values to choose from:

Authenticity	Equality	Humility	Loyalty	Responsibility
Adventure	Faith	Independence	Mindfulness	Security
Balance	Family	Integrity	Open-mindedness	Self-respect
Compassion	Freedom	Joy	Optimism	Service
Connection	Friendship	Justice	Patience	Spirituality
Courage	Fun	Kindness	Peace	Stability
Creativity	Gratitude	Knowledge	Perseverance	Strength
Dependability	Growth	Leadership	Purpose	Trust
Discipline	Honesty	Learning	Reliability	Wisdom
Empathy	Hope	Love	Respect	Responsibility

1.	6.
2.	7.
3.	8.
4.	9.
5.	10.

TOP 3 Values:

1. ______________________________

How does this value show up in your daily life and decisions?

____

____

____

____

2. ______________________________

How does this value show up in your daily life and decisions?

____

____

____

____

3. ______________________________

How does this value show up in your daily life and decisions?

____

____

____

____

thursday

The Impact of Core Beliefs on Relationships

The Impact of Core Beliefs on Relationships

Our core beliefs—those fundamental ideas we hold about ourselves, others, and the world—play a pivotal role in shaping not only how we view our own identity but also how we engage and relate with others. These beliefs act as an internal filter, influencing our expectations, communication patterns, and emotional responses in relationships. Understanding this impact is essential for anyone on the journey of exploring core beliefs and personal identity, as it offers insight into recurring relationship patterns and opens the door for healthier, more authentic connections.

Core beliefs typically develop early in life, shaped by family dynamics, cultural background, life experiences, and emotional events. For example, a child who experienced rejection or inconsistent affection may develop a core belief such as "I am unlovable" or "People cannot be trusted." These beliefs, often unconscious, continue to influence adult relationships in powerful ways. When we enter into relationships with these ingrained ideas, we may unknowingly seek evidence that confirms our beliefs—this is known as confirmation bias—and behave in ways that perpetuate the cycle. For instance, someone who believes they are unworthy of love might struggle with vulnerability, push others away, or settle for unhealthy relationships, thus reinforcing their core belief. Conversely, positive core beliefs, such as “I am worthy of love and respect,” tend to foster openness, trust, and mutual support.

The way core beliefs influence relationships extends beyond romantic connections. They affect friendships, family bonds, work relationships, and even casual social interactions. **Our beliefs determine how we interpret others' behaviors, how much we trust, and the boundaries we set.** Someone with a core belief of “I must always please others to be accepted” may find themselves overwhelmed and resentful, unable to assert their needs. Another person who believes “I can only rely on myself” may struggle to ask for help or to fully engage emotionally with others. These beliefs shape patterns of communication, attachment styles, and conflict resolution. Recognizing these influences can be transformative, as it allows individuals to identify which beliefs serve them well and which limit connection and intimacy.

The impact of core beliefs on relationships also highlights the importance of self-awareness and healing in personal growth. Often, relationship difficulties signal that our internal beliefs need attention. For example, repeated conflicts or feelings of loneliness might point to underlying beliefs about trust, worthiness, or safety. When we explore these roots, we gain insight into why we react as we do and can begin to shift unhelpful patterns. Therapy, self-reflection, and honest communication with loved ones are powerful tools for this work. **Healing core beliefs can increase emotional resilience, improve empathy, and foster healthier relational dynamics, enabling individuals to build relationships based on authenticity rather than fear or avoidance.**

Moreover, understanding the role of core beliefs encourages compassion—for ourselves and for others. **When we realize that difficult behaviors or misunderstandings often stem from deep-seated beliefs rather than malice, we can approach relationships with patience and kindness.** This perspective reduces blame and opens space for empathy, forgiveness, and growth. It also empowers individuals to choose relationships that affirm and nurture their evolving sense of self, rather than those that trigger old wounds or reinforce limiting beliefs.

In conclusion, core beliefs profoundly influence how we experience relationships and how relationships, in turn, shape our identity. **By exploring and understanding the origins and effects of these beliefs, we can break free from unconscious patterns that limit connection.** This journey not only deepens our self-awareness but also enhances our capacity to form meaningful, supportive, and authentic relationships. As we align our beliefs with our values and personal growth, we open ourselves to healthier relational experiences that reflect who we truly are and who we aspire to become.

Self-Assessment

The Impact of Core Beliefs on Relationships

Instructions: Rate each statement on a scale from 1 (Strongly Disagree) to 5 (Strongly Agree).

1. My core beliefs about myself influence how I behave in my relationships.
2. I notice patterns in my relationships that reflect beliefs I hold about trust and worthiness.
3. When I feel hurt or upset in relationships, I try to identify if a core belief is being triggered.
4. I find it challenging to form close relationships because of negative beliefs I have about myself.
5. I am aware of how my beliefs affect the boundaries I set with others.
6. My relationships improve when I work on changing limiting beliefs about myself.
7. I tend to attract people who confirm my core beliefs, whether positive or negative.
8. I feel capable of changing my core beliefs to create healthier relationships.

1 - Strongly Disagree	2 - Disagree	3 - Neutral /Unsure	4 - Agree	5 - Strongly Agree

Scoring Guide:

8–16:

You may be in the early stages of understanding how core beliefs affect your relationships. Consider exploring these beliefs more deeply.

17–28:

You have some awareness of this connection and may benefit from focused reflection and practice in challenging limiting beliefs.

29–40:

You are highly aware of the impact of core beliefs on your relationships and actively work to cultivate healthy, authentic connections.

Worksheet: Exploring How Core Beliefs Affect My Relationships

Step 1: Identify a Core Belief

Write down a core belief you have about yourself that you think influences your relationships.
Example: “I am not worthy of love” or “People will leave me if I’m vulnerable.”

My core belief:

____

____

____

____

Step 2: Reflect on Its Origin

Where do you think this belief came from? (Family, past experiences, culture, etc.)

____

____

____

____

Step 3: Notice Its Impact

How does this belief show up in your relationships? Consider your behavior, feelings, and interactions with others.

____

____

____

____

Step 4: Explore Emotional Responses

What emotions do you often feel in relationships that might be connected to this belief?

____

____

____

____

Step 5: Challenge and Reframe

Is this belief always true? What evidence do you have that contradicts it? Write a more balanced or positive belief to replace it.

Evidence against the belief:

____

____

____

____

New, empowering belief:

____

____

____

____

Step 6: Imagine Change

If you embraced this new belief, how might your relationships change?

____

____

____

____

Journal

1. Do I believe I am worthy of love? Why or why not?

2. What are my beliefs about trust and vulnerability?

3. How do I react when people get emotionally close?

Activity

The Importance of Recognizing Your Relationship Beliefs

Recognizing your relationship beliefs helps you understand how your past experiences, upbringing, and core values shape the way you connect with others. These beliefs often influence your expectations, boundaries, communication patterns, and emotional needs—sometimes without you even realizing it. By becoming aware of them, you can identify unhealthy patterns, challenge unrealistic expectations, and create healthier, more fulfilling relationships built on mutual respect, trust, and authenticity.

HOW TO: Relationship Belief Reflection

1. Write down a few recurring patterns in your relationships (e.g., pushing people away, becoming overly dependent).
2. For each, list the belief behind the behavior (e.g., "If I get too close, I'll get hurt").
3. Reflect: Are these beliefs still serving me? What could change?

Relationship Belief Reflection

Recurring Pattern	Belief Behind the Pattern	Is this Belief Still Serving me? What Could Change?

friday

Shifting Identity Through Growth and Recovery

Shifting Identity Through Growth and Recovery

Our identity is often thought of as a fixed set of traits or labels, but in reality, it is a dynamic and evolving construct. As we journey through life, particularly through processes of personal growth and recovery, our sense of who we are can—and often must—shift in profound ways. **Understanding how identity evolves allows us to explore the roots of our core beliefs, assess which ones still serve us, and cultivate a healthier, more authentic self. This exploration is critical for anyone committed to self-awareness and meaningful change.**

Growth and recovery—whether from trauma, addiction, mental health challenges, or life transitions—invite us to question and redefine our core beliefs. Often, these beliefs were formed in response to past circumstances, serving as survival mechanisms that helped us navigate difficult environments. For example, a person who experienced neglect may have adopted a belief that they are unworthy of love, a mindset that can severely limit their potential for connection and happiness. However, growth and recovery provide an opportunity to revisit these old beliefs with new awareness. By doing so, individuals can begin to separate their authentic self from the learned responses and narratives that no longer fit their lived experience or values.

This process of shifting identity is not simply about discarding old beliefs; it's about transformation. It involves integrating the lessons from past experiences with the present reality and future aspirations. **Recovery often includes recognizing patterns of thinking and behavior rooted in limiting core beliefs and consciously choosing new ways of being.** This might mean moving from a belief of "I am broken" to "I am healing and whole." Such shifts require patience, self-compassion, and sometimes professional support. Yet, the rewards are immense—a renewed sense of agency, resilience, and alignment between identity and authentic values.

As identity shifts through growth and recovery, individuals often encounter challenges, including feelings of uncertainty, loss, or discomfort. This is natural because change disrupts familiar patterns and requires navigating uncharted territory. For example, letting go of a long-held belief may temporarily create a sense of disorientation or vulnerability. However, these moments are crucial openings for deeper self-awareness and healing. **With support and reflection, people learn to**

embrace the fluidity of identity, understanding that evolving beliefs do not erase their past but enrich their narrative with complexity and hope.

Shifting identity also profoundly impacts relationships. As we change how we view ourselves, our interactions with others change too. **Recovery and growth can lead to setting healthier boundaries, choosing relationships that support our evolving values, and communicating with greater honesty and vulnerability.** Conversely, some relationships may no longer feel congruent with our new identity, prompting reassessment and, sometimes, difficult decisions. This relational shift is a vital aspect of aligning internal growth with external reality, fostering connections that affirm rather than diminish our authentic selves.

The importance of exploring the roots of our beliefs in this context cannot be overstated. When we understand where our core beliefs originated, we gain insight into why certain identities and behaviors emerged. This knowledge empowers us to consciously select which parts of our identity to carry forward and which to transform. It moves us from being passive recipients of past conditioning to active architects of our self-concept and life path.

Ultimately, shifting identity through growth and recovery is an ongoing journey—a lifelong process of becoming more fully who we are meant to be. **It honors the complexity of human experience, recognizing that identity is not static but a living, breathing reflection of our evolving understanding of self.** Embracing this process opens doors to greater authenticity, freedom, and connection, allowing us to live not according to limiting beliefs or old narratives but in alignment with our deepest truths.

Self-Assessment

Shifting Identity Through Growth and Recovery

Instructions: Rate each statement on a scale from 1 (Strongly Disagree) to 5 (Strongly Agree).

1. I recognize that my identity has changed over time as I've grown or healed.
2. I am aware of core beliefs I once held that I have since questioned or revised.
3. I feel comfortable exploring parts of myself that are unfamiliar or new.
4. I understand how past experiences have shaped my current beliefs and identity.
5. I actively work to replace limiting beliefs with healthier, more empowering ones.
6. Change in my sense of self sometimes feels uncomfortable, but necessary.
7. My relationships have shifted as I've grown and changed my beliefs.
8. I believe I have the ability to shape my identity intentionally as I recover and grow.

1 - Strongly Disagree	2 - Disagree	3 - Neutral /Unsure	4 - Agree	5 - Strongly Agree

Scoring Guide:

8–16: You may be beginning to recognize identity shifts. Consider exploring your growth and recovery journey with curiosity and support.

17–28: You have some awareness and are engaging with the process of evolving your identity and beliefs.

29–40: You are actively embracing and shaping your identity through growth and recovery, using this awareness to foster positive change.

Worksheet: Who Am I Becoming?

Exploring Shifts in Identity Through Growth and Recovery

1. Old Beliefs and Identities

List a few core beliefs or identity labels you once held that no longer feel true or helpful to you.

(Examples: “I’m a failure,” “I always have to be strong,” “I don’t matter,” “I’m just an addict.”)

How did these beliefs form? (Think about family, culture, past experiences, trauma, etc.)

2. Letting Go & Letting Grow

Which belief(s) or identity pieces are you working to let go of in your growth or recovery process?

What makes it hard to let them go?

What do you hope to make space for as you release these beliefs?

3. New Identity Insights

List some new beliefs, values, or identity traits you are beginning to embrace. (Examples: "I am healing," "I am worthy," "I can ask for help," "I'm becoming more authentic.")

How do these feel different from your past beliefs?

4. Relationships & Growth

How have your evolving beliefs impacted your relationships?

Are there relationships that support your new identity? Which ones might feel misaligned now?

____
____
____
____

5. Affirming Your Becoming

Complete the following sentences:

I am learning that I am...

____
____
____
____

A part of me that's growing stronger is...

____
____
____
____

In my recovery/growth, I want to be known as someone who...

____
____
____
____

Journal

1. How has my sense of identity changed in the past year?

2. What am I letting go of? What am I stepping into?

3. Who am I becoming?

Activity

The Importance of Creating a "Then, Now, Next" Identity Chart

Creating a "Then, Now, Next" identity chart helps you reflect on how your identity has evolved over time and where you're headed. By examining who you were, who you are now, and who you want to become, you can recognize patterns of growth, release limiting labels, and set intentional goals for your future self. This visual process encourages self-awareness, empowerment, and a deeper understanding of how your experiences shape your journey toward healing and purpose.

HOW TO: "Then, Now, Next" Identity Chart

Create a chart with the following columns:

- Timeframe
- Description of Self
- Beliefs Held
- New or Emerging Beliefs

"Then, Now, Next" Identity Chart

Timeframe	Description of Self	Beliefs Held	New or Emerging Beliefs

Vicki

Personal Recovery Story

I began using alcohol in college, but it wasn't until my mid-20s that I realized I was drinking more than most of the people around me. I wasn't drinking daily, but I noticed I wasn't capable of just "having a few drinks." Every time I did drink, it was to the point of blacking out or passing out. As the years went by, my drinking increased to dangerous and unsustainable levels. I was drinking every day—before work, after work, socially, anti-socially. It got to the point where I needed a drink when I woke up in the morning just to calm my trembling hands. My behavior was beyond reprehensible throughout the course of my active addiction—I racked up 2 DUIs, lost more than one job, and treated my friends and family horribly. After years of "hiding" it (I use quotes because I was fooling no one but myself), I finally checked into treatment.

I would love for my treatment story to be "I went to treatment and lived happily ever after," but I hit a few stumbling blocks along the way. After completing my first residential treatment program, I was doing well. I managed to stay sober for a few years, got married, and had a beautiful daughter. Everything was great until my marriage started to implode. I was depressed and anxious all the time, my self-esteem took a tumble, and I had all but forgotten how to use my healthy coping mechanisms, so I turned back to alcohol as a crutch. Although things never got quite as bad as they did prior to treatment, living my life this way and putting my daughter's safety in jeopardy was unacceptable. I went back to treatment, this time much further away from home. I didn't want my life to become a cycle of being in and out of rehab centers, so I needed this time to stick. I stayed for six weeks, then entered an outpatient program while staying in a sober living house for an additional six weeks. I learned to live a normal daily existence without alcohol, reinforced my coping mechanisms, learned some new coping mechanisms, built back my self-esteem, and took a deep dive into why I had such a lack of self-worth. I attended twice-weekly therapy sessions and went to several 12-step meetings per week. After completing the outpatient program and returning home, I continued seeing a therapist weekly and went to AA on a regular basis. I credit the treatment center, IOP program, therapists, AA, and even myself for the ongoing success I've had in remaining sober and living a fulfilling life!

Today, I'm proud to say I have been in recovery for over 7.5 years. Additionally, I went back to college to become an addiction counselor! Through ongoing self-discovery in therapy, I have learned why I think the way I do and the way my personal history has shaped my emotions and decisions. Understanding my inner self has been instrumental in my ability to make better choices. My story is long, winding, and incredibly messy, but I wouldn't change a thing about it—it has made me a better mom, daughter, friend, and overall person. Having been through the rough times has made the good times even better. My future looks sunny, and I can't wait to see what comes next!

Final Thoughts

Reclaiming Identity Through Core Belief Exploration

As we close this chapter, it becomes clear that our core beliefs—whether shaped by early experiences, trauma, family dynamics, or societal messaging—form the foundation of our identity. These beliefs impact not only how we view ourselves, but also how we relate to others, how we make choices, and how we navigate life. **By identifying and examining both internal and external triggers, we begin to understand the patterns that reinforce limiting beliefs and emotional reactions. This awareness creates space for healing, regulation, and intentional change.**

Through the processes of challenging limiting beliefs and clarifying our values, we gain the insight needed to shift from living on autopilot to living in alignment with who we truly are. Values help anchor our identity, offering clarity about what matters most and what kind of person we want to be. As we grow and recover, our identity begins to shift—not by discarding our past, but by integrating it with compassion. **This transformation allows us to shed old narratives of shame, fear, or inadequacy and replace them with self-worth, agency, and authenticity.**

Ultimately, exploring core beliefs and identity is a journey of rediscovery and reconnection. It invites us to return to ourselves, choose what beliefs we want to carry forward, and live in a way that reflects our truest values and intentions. The impact of this work is deeply personal yet profoundly relational—improving our well-being, strengthening our relationships, and empowering us to live with clarity, courage, and purpose. This chapter is not the end, but a foundation for ongoing growth, healing, and becoming.

Reflection

1. **Who am I beneath the labels I've worn or the roles I've played?**
   Write freely without worrying about titles, achievements, or failures. Let your truth emerge.

2. **What beliefs about myself did I learn growing up that may no longer serve me today?**
   Were you told you had to be strong, quiet, perfect, or invisible? Where did those messages come from?

3. **When in my life have I felt most *me*—authentic, free, and alive?**
   Describe those moments. What were you doing? Who were you with? How can you invite more of that feeling into your life now?

Saturday

Mindful Movement & Nature Connection

Weekend Work

Reconnecting with your body and the natural world is a powerful way to ground yourself in the present moment and promote healing in recovery. **Nature offers a calming, nonjudgmental space that helps reduce stress, quiet racing thoughts, and restore emotional balance.** Engaging in mindful movement like walking, stretching, or simply breathing fresh air can reawaken your senses and strengthen the mind-body connection that may have been neglected during active addiction. This reconnection encourages self-awareness, inner peace, and a deeper appreciation for life's simple, healing rhythms.

Goal:

Reconnect with your body and the natural world to promote mental clarity and emotional regulation.

Activities:

- Group hike or nature walk
- Outdoor yoga or tai chi session
- Journaling in a scenic location
- Nature scavenger hunt (solo or group)

10 Nature Activities I would Like to Try:
•
•
•
•
•
•
•
•
•
•

sunday

Process, Recharge, Reset, and Reflect

The Importance of Rest: To Process, Recharge, Reset, and Reflect- Part 1

Rest is not a reward for hard work—it is an essential part of it. In today's go-go-go culture, rest is often undervalued or misunderstood as laziness. But true rest is what allows the mind, body, and spirit to process experiences, regain energy, and re-engage with purpose. **It is in stillness that we begin to understand the deeper layers of our journey, the meaning behind our struggles, and the wisdom hidden in our experiences.**

Processing takes time and space. When we are constantly in motion, it's easy to gloss over emotions or avoid confronting difficult truths. **Rest gives the nervous system a break and allows the brain to sort through thoughts, memories, and emotions in a less reactive state.** Whether through sleep, solitude, nature, or quiet reflection, these slower moments create room for healing and clarity that busy days cannot provide.

2

Understanding your triggers and patterns

Introduction

Understanding your triggers and patterns is an essential step toward personal growth and emotional well-being. Triggers are experiences or situations—either internal (like thoughts, memories, or physical sensations) or external (such as places, people, or events)—that spark intense emotional or behavioral responses. Many of our reactions are rooted in past trauma or learned behaviors, making certain situations feel overwhelming or out of our control. Recognizing the difference between internal and external triggers allows you to develop more insight into your emotional world, helping you respond with awareness rather than reaction.

By identifying emotional and behavioral patterns, you begin to notice the early warning signs that something is off—such as tension in your body, racing thoughts, or sudden mood shifts. These cues serve as valuable indicators to pause and choose a different response. **Developing healthy coping strategies and alternatives—like grounding techniques, journaling, physical movement, or reaching out for support—can interrupt harmful cycles and support healing.** This self-awareness empowers you to break free from automatic responses and take meaningful steps toward emotional regulation and lasting change.

Objective

The objective of this section is to help individuals gain a deeper understanding of their emotional triggers and behavior patterns. By exploring the difference between internal and external triggers, recognizing the impact of trauma and learned responses, and identifying early warning signs and emotional cues, individuals can begin to build greater self-awareness. This awareness lays the foundation for developing effective coping strategies and healthy alternatives that support emotional regulation, personal empowerment, and long-term recovery or growth.

W2: Agenda

M — Types of Triggers: Internal VS External

T — The Role of Trauma and Learned Responses

W — Recognizing Emotional and Behavioral Patterns

T — Early Warning Signs and Emotional Cues

F — Coping Strategies and Healthy Alternatives

S — Creative Expression & Self Discovery

Monday

Understanding Triggers: Internal vs. External

Understanding Triggers: Internal vs. External

Exploring the Roots of Our Beliefs and Sense of Self

When we begin to explore our core beliefs and identity, one essential area to examine is our emotional triggers—those moments when something outside or inside of us sets off a powerful emotional reaction. **Understanding our triggers helps reveal where our beliefs come from, how they've been shaped by experience, and how they influence our identity today.** This process requires curiosity and compassion, not judgment. Triggers are not signs of weakness; they are invitations to uncover deeper truths about what we've experienced, what we've internalized, and how we can begin to heal.

Triggers fall into two primary categories: internal and external. Internal triggers originate from within. They might include a sudden memory, intrusive thoughts, bodily sensations (like tightness in the chest or a racing heart), or even a vague emotional wave that seems to come out of nowhere. These triggers are often the most confusing because they don't always have an obvious cause, yet they can strongly affect how we feel and behave. For example, someone might feel a sudden sense of shame or fear after making a small mistake—this reaction may not come from the current situation but from internalized beliefs formed in childhood, such as "I'm not good enough" or "I always mess things up." These beliefs are often rooted in past emotional experiences and reinforced over time until they become a part of our identity.

On the other hand, external triggers come from the world around us. These can include specific people, places, objects, smells, sounds, or situations that are associated—often unconsciously—with past experiences. For instance, a raised voice might instantly trigger anxiety in someone who grew up in a household with yelling and conflict. A smell or song might bring on sudden sadness if it's connected to a loss or difficult memory. External triggers often catch us off guard, especially when we aren't aware of the connection between the current moment and a past emotional wound. These responses are not random; they are clues pointing to unfinished emotional business. When we pay attention to these reactions, we start to see how our environment influences our inner world—and vice versa.

Understanding the difference between internal and external triggers can help us begin to trace emotional reactions back to their source. This is where we start to uncover the roots of our core beliefs—the deeply held assumptions we carry about ourselves, others, and the world. If certain triggers cause us to feel rejected, afraid, or unworthy, they may be exposing a belief like "I'm not lovable," "I have to be perfect to be accepted," or "The world isn't safe." These beliefs were often formed early in life and may have been based on real experiences of pain, neglect, or trauma. However, just because a belief has been with us for a long time doesn't mean it's true or helpful today. **Exploring our triggers offers a pathway to challenge and reshape these beliefs.**

As we become more aware of our personal triggers, we also begin to reconnect with our authentic identity—the version of ourselves that exists underneath the defenses, fears, and old patterns. **Recognizing and naming our triggers gives us the power to pause before reacting, choose different responses, and act in alignment with who we truly are—not who we were told to be or who we learned to be in order to survive.** This kind of self-awareness strengthens our ability to live with integrity and clarity. We begin to respond with curiosity instead of shame and compassion instead of self-criticism. In this way, identifying our triggers isn't just a coping skill—it's a doorway to deeper healing and self-discovery.

In summary, understanding internal and external triggers helps illuminate the hidden beliefs we've internalized and how they influence our identity. These triggers serve as emotional signposts that can guide us toward greater self-awareness, emotional resilience, and personal empowerment. **Rather than fearing our reactions, we can learn from them, trace them back to their origin, and gently begin to rewrite the stories we tell ourselves.** This exploration creates the foundation for a more grounded, authentic sense of self—one that is shaped not by old wounds, but by intention, healing, and truth.

Self-Assessment

Identifying Internal vs. External Triggers

Instructions: Rate each statement on a scale from *1* (Strongly Disagree) to *5* (Strongly Agree).

1. I can recognize when an internal thought or memory is triggering a strong emotional reaction.
2. Physical sensations in my body (e.g., tightness, racing heart) alert me to being triggered before I notice external events.
3. External events or situations (like people, places, or sounds) often cause me to feel triggered.
4. I am able to distinguish whether my emotional reaction is caused by something inside me or something outside of me.
5. I notice early warning signs in my body or mind that indicate I am being triggered.
6. When triggered, I am aware if the cause is an internal experience (thought, memory, sensation) rather than something external.
7. I feel more in control of my responses to external triggers than internal ones.
8. I have strategies to manage both internal and external triggers effectively.

1 – Strongly Disagree	2 – Disagree	3 – Neutral /Unsure	4 – Agree	5 – Strongly Agree

Scoring Guide:

8–16: Low awareness of your triggers; consider focusing on identifying internal and external signals.

17–28: Moderate awareness; there is room to deepen understanding and response skills.

29–40: High awareness and good recognition of your triggers and how they impact you.

Worksheet: Identifying Your Internal and External Triggers

Instructions:

Take your time to thoughtfully answer each question below. Use specific examples from your recent experiences to deepen your understanding of your emotional triggers.

____

____

____

____

1. Describe a recent time when a thought or memory triggered a strong emotional reaction. *Was this trigger internal (from within you) or external (from your environment)?*

____

____

____

____

2. Which affects you more strongly: physical sensations in your body (e.g., tightness, nausea) or events/situations happening around you? *Explain your answer.*

____

____

____

____

3. Recall a moment when you felt anxious, upset, or overwhelmed. Was the trigger something outside of you (like a person or place) or inside (like a worry or flashback)?
Describe the situation.

____

____

4. When you feel triggered, do you notice physical signs first (like racing heart, sweating, or muscle tension) before realizing what caused it?

Yes

No

Sometimes

If yes or sometimes, describe what sensations you notice.

5. List any people, places, or situations that consistently provoke strong emotional reactions for you.

6. Do certain thoughts, memories, or feelings come up unexpectedly and cause intense emotions without an obvious external cause? *Describe one example.*

7. How do you usually respond when you notice an internal trigger (like a negative thought or sensation)? How about an external trigger?

8. Reflecting on your triggers, do you feel you have more control or awareness over your internal triggers or external triggers? Why?

Reflection:

What new insights did you gain about your triggers by completing this worksheet? How might this awareness help you respond differently in the future?

Journal

1. What are three internal triggers I notice most often?

2. Describe a recent situation where an external trigger led to a strong emotional reaction.

3. What patterns do I see in the places, people, or situations that affect me?

Activity

The Importance of Creating a Trigger Map

Creating a trigger map allows you to visually identify and understand the people, places, situations, and emotions that tend to activate your stress responses or unhealthy behaviors. By mapping out these triggers, you gain clarity on the patterns that disrupt your well-being and can begin developing healthier coping strategies. This process increases emotional awareness, supports relapse prevention, and empowers you to navigate challenges with greater control and confidence.

HOW TO: Create a Trigger Map

1. Draw a line down a page—label one side "Internal" and the other "External."
2. List as many personal triggers as you can under each.
3. Reflect on which ones you can control, avoid, or prepare for.

Trigger Map

Internal Triggers	External Triggers

Which ones can you control, avoid, or prepare for?

Chris

Personal Recovery Story

I was using methamphetamine and cocaine. I was using cocaine every day for about 2-3 years, and then I got introduced to methamphetamine, and I started using that every day for 20 years. It affected my life in ways I couldn't even imagine and led me to do things I would never have imagined I would do. I started selling drugs and having women work under me (if you know what I mean), and I was paying hotel owners in drugs to be able to stay in the hotel and letting women work out of the hotel room. I lost most contact with my three kids and the family that did support me. I lost cars, apartments, jobs, and friends throughout my addiction.

The approach that worked for me was when I got arrested on June 5, 2024—the day of my mama's birthday. I had a warrant when I got stopped, and I had a bus ticket to go up to Prescott Valley to a rehab center on June 6, 2024. I was sentenced to 6 months if I got into a program. I was accepted into a program in the Phoenix area, and I got off of IPS 3 months early. The breaking point was when the judge said that if I come back again on any charges, she was giving me 10 years flat in DOC. My mom was in the courtroom and told me to call her when I got back to my pod. When I called her, this is what she told me: "If you go to prison, Christopher Maurice Palmer, I will send you money, but I will never come visit you because I can't see my only son behind bars like you had to see your father your whole life." I broke down and cried. I truly attempted to get sober about 4 times, where I actually did the work. Working a program and then transitioning into a sober living is what worked for me.

My life in recovery now is amazing. I have a great job, and I have relationships that I would have never thought I would ever have again. My two boys and I have the best relationship we could ever have. I mean, they call me with all their problems, and they know I will answer and give them my opinion, and I don't sugarcoat anything I tell them. I am currently a House Manager, and I told myself that I would work for them while I was attending their program. I have the best relationship with my mom, and she trusts me now. She knows I am going to show up. I will say this: the most positive thing I recognize about myself in my recovery is that I am PRESENT IN THE MOMENT! My uncle always told me you can have all the money in the world, but the best thing in life is the TIME you spend with family and friends. My recovery date is June 6, 2024, and it's the day after my mama's birthday, so every year I get to celebrate her day and then my day when I changed my whole life for the better.

tuesday

The Role of Trauma and Learned Responses

The Role of Trauma and Learned Responses

Exploring Triggers and the Roots of Our Beliefs

Understanding your emotional triggers and behavioral patterns begins with recognizing the profound role trauma and learned responses play in shaping how you think, feel, and react to the world. **Trauma is not just about catastrophic events—it can also come from subtle, repeated experiences where your emotional needs were unmet, your safety was threatened, or your sense of worth was challenged.** These moments leave imprints on the nervous system and often lead to automatic responses that become deeply wired into your behavior. Over time, the body and mind learn how to protect you by reacting quickly to perceived danger—even when that danger is no longer present. This is the foundation of many emotional triggers.

When trauma occurs, the brain stores the experience as a memory, not just in thoughts but also in the body. The nervous system remembers the sights, sounds, smells, and sensations tied to the moment of fear or pain. Later, when something in the present—an internal sensation or an external event—resembles that original moment, the body reacts as if the threat is happening again. This is why people may feel intense fear, anger, or sadness in situations that seem objectively harmless. The reaction is not about the current moment; it's about the unresolved emotional memory that has been activated. **These automatic responses are not chosen—they are learned patterns of survival.** Understanding this helps shift the narrative from "What's wrong with me?" to "What happened to me?"

Learned responses develop as a way to adapt to emotionally overwhelming or unsafe environments. For example, a child who grows up in a household where emotional expression is punished may learn to suppress their feelings to avoid conflict. Over time, this suppression becomes a pattern, and the person may struggle to express needs or set boundaries as an adult. Similarly, someone who experienced rejection might learn to people-please or overachieve to feel worthy of love. These coping mechanisms once served a purpose—they helped you survive. But in adulthood, they often become limiting and prevent you from forming authentic relationships or living in alignment with your true self. By examining these patterns, you begin to uncover the beliefs formed in those early experiences, such as "I'm only lovable if I'm useful" or "My feelings don't matter."

The connection between trauma, learned responses, and emotional triggers is essential in understanding the roots of your beliefs. Triggers are like emotional alarms that signal a belief is being activated—usually one tied to an old wound. A raised voice might trigger the belief "I'm in danger." Being left out of a group might activate the belief "I'm not good enough." These responses are not just emotional—they are reflections of the stories we've been telling ourselves, often without realizing it. By recognizing what triggers you and what responses you've learned, you gain the power to question those beliefs. Are they true now? Do they serve you today? This process opens the door to rewriting your inner narrative.

Ultimately, exploring the role of trauma and learned responses is not about blaming the past—it's about reclaiming your future. When you understand why you react the way you do, you begin to develop compassion for yourself. **You see that your patterns were protective, not defective.** And with that compassion comes the ability to change. You can begin to replace automatic reactions with intentional responses. You can learn new ways to soothe your nervous system, challenge old beliefs, and show up in your life from a place of self-awareness rather than survival. This is the heart of healing—transforming unconscious patterns into conscious choices. Understanding your triggers and the role of trauma helps you not only manage emotions but also reconnect with who you truly are beneath the layers of defense and adaptation.

Self-Assessment

Understanding Trauma and Learned Responses

Instructions: Rate each statement on a scale from *1* (Strongly Disagree) to *5* (Strongly Agree).

1. I recognize that many of my emotional reactions today come from past traumatic or difficult experiences.
2. When I feel triggered, I understand that my response might be a learned pattern developed for survival.
3. I am aware of specific behaviors I use that were originally coping mechanisms, but may no longer serve me well.
4. I find it helpful to explore how my early life experiences influence my current beliefs and feelings.
5. I can identify situations where my trauma has shaped my beliefs about myself or others.
6. I notice when my reactions are automatic and linked to past pain rather than the present situation.
7. I am open to challenging and changing old beliefs that were formed through trauma or learned responses.
8. I use strategies or seek support to manage the impact of trauma on my emotional responses.

1 - Strongly Disagree	2 - Disagree	3 - Neutral /Unsure	4 - Agree	5 - Strongly Agree

Scoring Guide:

8–16: You may benefit from learning more about how trauma affects emotions and behaviors.

17–28: Moderate understanding; increasing awareness of trauma's impact.

29–40: Strong awareness and active engagement with healing trauma and changing patterns.

Worksheet: Exploring the Role of Trauma and Learned Responses

Instructions: Rate each statement on a scale from 1 (Strongly Disagree) to 5 (Strongly Agree).

Scale: 1 = Strongly Disagree | 2 = Disagree | 3 = Neutral | 4 = Agree | 5 = Strongly Agree

1. I recognize that many of my emotional reactions today come from past traumatic or difficult experiences.

1 2 3 4 5

____

____

____

____

2. When I feel triggered, I understand that my response might be a learned pattern developed for survival.

1 2 3 4 5

____

____

____

____

3. I am aware of specific behaviors I use that were originally coping mechanisms but may no longer serve me well.

1 2 3 4 5

____

____

____

____

4. I find it helpful to explore how my early life experiences influence my current beliefs and feelings.

1 2 3 4 5

____

____

5. I can identify situations where my trauma has shaped my beliefs about myself or others.

1 2 3 4 5

6. I notice when my reactions are automatic and linked to past pain rather than the present situation.

1 2 3 4 5

7. I am open to challenging and changing old beliefs that were formed through trauma or learned responses.

1 2 3 4 5

8. I use strategies or seek support to manage the impact of trauma on my emotional responses.

1 2 3 4 5

Reflection Questions:

- What did you learn about yourself through this assessment?
- Which areas do you feel strongest in? Which could use more attention?
- How might understanding trauma and learned responses help you change old patterns?
- What is one small step you can take to begin healing or managing your triggers better?

Journal

1. **What is one reaction I have that feels bigger than the situation? Where might it come from?**

2. **How did my past experiences teach me to react this way?**

3. **When I get triggered, what younger version of myself might be responding?**

Activity

The Importance of Creating a Personal Timeline (Triggers)

Creating a personal timeline focused on triggers helps you trace significant life events that have shaped your emotional responses and coping patterns. By visually organizing past experiences alongside the emotions and behaviors they sparked, you can begin to see connections between unresolved pain and present-day challenges. This process fosters deeper self-awareness, validates your journey, and opens the door to healing by helping you understand the roots of your triggers and how they've impacted your life.

HOW TO: Timeline Reflection

Create a personal timeline highlighting difficult or formative experiences. Then note current triggers that may link back to those moments. Circle patterns or events that still hold emotional weight.

Timeline Reflection

Difficult or Formative Experiences	Is there a current trigger linking to this moment?

wednesday

Recognizing Emotional and Behavioral Patterns

Recognizing Emotional and Behavioral Patterns

Understanding Triggers to Explore the Roots of Your Beliefs

Emotional and behavioral patterns are the rhythms and reactions we repeat—often without realizing it—in response to the world around and within us. These patterns are deeply connected to the triggers we experience, whether internal (like thoughts, memories, or bodily sensations) or external (such as interactions, environments, or stressful events). When we take time to notice our emotional and behavioral patterns, we begin to uncover the deeper beliefs that have been quietly shaping our lives. These beliefs often stem from past experiences and become the lens through which we interpret new ones. **Recognizing these cycles is not about blaming yourself, but about becoming more conscious of what drives your reactions and how you can shift them.**

Our emotional patterns typically develop early in life as responses to unmet needs, fear, or repeated emotional pain. For example, if you experienced criticism or rejection frequently, you may have learned to react to conflict with withdrawal, defensiveness, or anxiety. Over time, this becomes an emotional loop—whenever you perceive tension or disapproval, your body and brain react in the same familiar way, even if the situation isn't truly dangerous. Similarly, behavioral patterns like avoiding difficult conversations, overcommitting to please others, or shutting down emotionally are often connected to old survival strategies. These behaviors may feel automatic because they were once necessary to keep you emotionally safe. But in the present, they may no longer serve you.

Triggers are the sparks that activate these patterns. A tone of voice, a missed text, or even a passing comment might trigger a disproportionate emotional reaction. That's because what's really being activated is not the present moment—it's the belief underneath. If your core belief is "I'm not enough," then being left out of a conversation can feel like rejection, even if it wasn't meant that way. If you carry the belief "I'm responsible for everyone's happiness," then someone else's bad mood might trigger anxiety and guilt. Recognizing these patterns helps you ask key questions: What am I feeling? When have I felt this way before? What belief is being activated? With practice, you can start to differentiate between what's happening now and what old story might be shaping your response.

The ability to recognize and reflect on emotional and behavioral patterns is essential for growth and healing. These patterns are the fingerprints of your inner belief system—they reveal the narratives you've been living by. By slowing down and observing how you typically react when stressed, overwhelmed, or triggered, you gain valuable insight into yourself. You might notice, for instance, that you tend to shut down in the face of conflict or become overly accommodating when you sense someone is upset. These aren't random reactions—they are strategies you've learned over time, based on beliefs like "My needs don't matter," "If I speak up, I'll be abandoned," or "I have to be perfect to be loved." Recognizing the emotional roots of these patterns gives you the power to begin changing them.

Ultimately, understanding your emotional and behavioral patterns is an act of self-awareness and self-compassion. Instead of seeing your reactions as flaws, you begin to view them as clues—messages from the parts of you that still feel vulnerable, hurt, or unseen. The more you pay attention to these patterns, the more you can interrupt them and choose responses that align with your true values rather than your past pain. You begin to rewrite the story you tell yourself about who you are and how you're allowed to show up in the world. This doesn't happen overnight, but with reflection, intention, and support, you can begin to shift out of survival mode and into a space where authenticity, clarity, and emotional freedom can grow.

Self-Assessment

Recognizing Emotional and Behavioral Patterns

Instructions: Rate each statement on a scale from *1* (Strongly Disagree) to *5* (Strongly Agree).

1. I am aware of recurring emotional reactions I experience in similar situations.
2. I can identify behaviors I repeat when I feel stressed or triggered.
3. I notice when my emotional responses are disproportionate to the current situation.
4. I recognize patterns where I tend to shut down, avoid, or withdraw emotionally.
5. I am able to see when I react impulsively or habitually without thinking.
6. I understand how my past experiences influence the way I behave in relationships.
7. I can identify beliefs that drive my emotional and behavioral patterns.
8. I actively reflect on my emotional patterns to improve my responses and interactions.

1 – Strongly Disagree	2 – Disagree	3 – Neutral /Unsure	4 – Agree	5 – Strongly Agree

Scoring Guide:

8–16: Low awareness of your emotional and behavioral patterns; consider paying closer attention to your reactions.

17–28: Moderate awareness; some recognition of patterns but room for deeper exploration.

29–40: High awareness and insight into your emotional and behavioral cycles.

Worksheet: Recognizing Emotional and Behavioral Patterns

Instructions:
Take time to thoughtfully answer each question. Be honest and curious—this is an opportunity to better understand the patterns that shape your emotional responses and behaviors.

1. What emotional reactions do you notice showing up repeatedly in your life (e.g., anger, anxiety, sadness, shutting down)? In what types of situations do they usually appear?

____

____

____

____

2. Are there behaviors you find yourself doing automatically when you're overwhelmed, hurt, or stressed? What are they?

____

____

____

____

3. Think about a recent situation where your reaction felt bigger than the moment required. What triggered you, and how did you respond?

____

____

____

____

4. What patterns do you notice in how you handle conflict, disappointment, or criticism?

____

____

5. Do you notice any patterns in how you relate to others emotionally (e.g., needing reassurance, withdrawing, people-pleasing, avoiding vulnerability)?

6. Can you connect any of these patterns to earlier experiences or relationships in your life? What beliefs might have formed as a result?

7. Which of your emotional or behavioral patterns feels helpful or protective? Which feels limiting or harmful?

8. What is one small change you'd like to make the next time you notice a familiar emotional or behavioral pattern showing up?

Journal

1. What does my body feel like when I'm starting to get overwhelmed?

2. What are three signs I'm emotionally off balance?

3. What can I do when I notice these signs?

Activity

The Importance of Recognizing Patterns

Tracking patterns helps you recognize recurring thoughts, emotions, behaviors, and triggers that influence your daily life. By paying attention to these cycles, you can identify what supports your well-being and what leads to setbacks or distress. This awareness empowers you to break harmful habits, reinforce positive choices, and make more intentional decisions that align with your goals and values. It's a powerful tool for personal growth, emotional regulation, and lasting change.

HOW TO: Pattern Tracker

For one week, track one recurring emotional or behavioral pattern.

Note what happened before, how you felt, what you did, and how you felt after.

Reflect on insights gained at the end of the week.

Pattern Tracker

Which recurring emotional or behavioral pattern will be tracked:

____

Day	What happened before	How do you feel?	What did you do to regulate?	How do you feel after?
Monday				
Tuesday				
Wednesday				
Thursday				
Friday				
Saturday				
Sunday				

What insight did you gain?

____

____

____

____

Early Warning Signs and Emotional Cues

Early Warning Signs and Emotional Cues

Learning to Recognize the Body's Language and the Stories Beneath

Understanding your triggers and patterns means learning to listen to your body and emotions more closely than you may be used to. One of the most powerful ways to do this is by becoming aware of early warning signs and emotional cues—subtle (and sometimes not-so-subtle) indicators that your nervous system is becoming activated. These signals can show up as physical sensations, shifts in mood, changes in thought patterns, or even sudden urges to act or shut down. While they may seem inconvenient or disruptive in the moment, they are actually protective messengers trying to alert you to a deeper emotional need or past experience being reawakened.

Early warning signs are often the body's first attempt to communicate that something is off. These might include clenched jaws, a racing heart, sweaty palms, restlessness, or a pit in the stomach. For others, warning signs can be more cognitive or emotional: spiraling thoughts, irritability, numbness, confusion, or a strong urge to escape. These signs are often linked to internal or external triggers—an unkind comment, a certain tone of voice, a memory, or even a quiet moment where difficult thoughts arise. In many cases, the warning signs begin before we even consciously realize we're being triggered. That's why developing awareness of your body's signals is essential in creating space between stimulus and response.

Emotional cues are the feelings that accompany or follow these physical and behavioral signs. They may include sadness, anger, fear, shame, guilt, or anxiety. While these emotions may feel intense or overwhelming, they are not random—they are tied to the stories and beliefs we've learned about ourselves. For example, a feeling of sadness might arise when a core belief like "I'm not important" is triggered by being excluded from a conversation. Anger might surface when you believe "I'm being taken advantage of again." Fear might show up when you feel like your value or safety is being threatened. Each emotion is tied to an interpretation—and those interpretations are shaped by our past experiences and the beliefs that came from them.

By learning to recognize early warning signs and emotional cues, you begin to interrupt automatic, unconscious patterns. You start to notice the moment tension begins to rise instead of waiting until you've already reacted. That pause creates room for choice. Rather than snapping, shutting down, or people-pleasing, you can ask yourself: What am I feeling right now? What might this emotion be trying to tell me? What belief is being activated? These small questions open up a deeper level of self-inquiry that helps you get closer to the roots of your emotional reactions. Often, the answer leads back to a core belief formed in childhood or in a past painful experience. With this awareness, you can begin to question whether that belief still fits your life today—and begin the process of rewriting it.

Ultimately, recognizing early warning signs and emotional cues is about building a trusting relationship with yourself. These signals are not your enemy—they are part of your inner guidance system. When you pay attention to them, you begin to meet your emotional needs with care instead of criticism, and respond to your triggers with clarity instead of chaos. Over time, this practice helps you become less reactive and more grounded in who you truly are. It empowers you to understand your emotional world and the beliefs that drive it—so you can move through life with greater self-awareness, intention, and compassion.

Self-Assessment

Early Warning Signs and Emotional Cues

Instructions: Rate each statement on a scale from *1* (Strongly Disagree) to *5* (Strongly Agree).

1. I can recognize physical signs (like tension, rapid heartbeat, or restlessness) that signal I'm becoming emotionally activated.
2. I notice changes in my thinking (such as racing thoughts or negative self-talk) when I'm starting to feel triggered.
3. I am aware of emotional cues (like sadness, anger, or fear) before my reaction becomes intense.
4. I can usually identify what I am feeling in the early stages of emotional discomfort.
5. I know the types of situations or interactions that tend to bring on early signs of emotional stress.
6. I often realize I'm emotionally triggered only *after* I've reacted. *(reverse scored)*
7. I pay attention to patterns in my body and emotions to catch when I'm starting to feel overwhelmed.
8. I use early emotional or physical signs as a cue to slow down or use a coping strategy.

1 –	2 –	3 –	4 –	5 –
Strongly Disagree	Disagree	Neutral /Unsure	Agree	Strongly Agree

Scoring Guide:

(Reverse score question #6 by subtracting your rating from 6 before totaling)

8–16: Low awareness of early emotional and physical signs – consider practicing body scanning and emotional check-ins.

17–28: Moderate awareness – you're noticing some cues but may miss others; focus on slowing down in moments of stress.

29–40: Strong awareness – you're attuned to your signals and likely able to intervene before escalation.

Worksheet: Early Warning Signs and Emotional Cues

Instructions:
Read each statement below and circle the number that best describes how true it feels for you. Then reflect on your answers in the space provided.

Scale: *1* = Strongly Disagree *2* = Disagree *3* = Neutral *4* = Agree *5* = Strongly Agree

1. I can recognize physical signs (like tension, rapid heartbeat, or restlessness) that signal I'm becoming emotionally activated.

1 2 3 4 5

2. I notice changes in my thinking (such as racing thoughts or negative self-talk) when I'm starting to feel triggered.

1 2 3 4 5

3. I am aware of emotional cues (like sadness, anger, or fear) before my reaction becomes intense.

1 2 3 4 5

4. I can usually identify what I am feeling in the early stages of emotional discomfort.

1 2 3 4 5

---

5. I know the types of situations or interactions that tend to bring on early signs of emotional stress.

1 2 3 4 5

---

6. I often realize I'm emotionally triggered only after I've reacted.

1 2 3 4 5

(Reverse scored—subtract your answer from 6 before adding your total)

---

7. I pay attention to patterns in my body and emotions to catch when I'm starting to feel overwhelmed.

1 2 3 4 5

---

8. I use early emotional or physical signs as a cue to slow down or use a coping strategy.

1 2 3 4 5

____

____

____

____

Scoring:

Add your scores (remember to reverse score question *6*):

Total: ______ / *40*

8–16: You may not yet recognize the early signs of emotional overwhelm—try practicing body scans or emotional check-ins.

17–28: You're starting to tune in, but there's room to deepen awareness.

29–40: Strong awareness—you are likely able to catch triggers early and respond effectivelyw

Journal

1. What does my body feel like when I'm starting to get overwhelmed?

2. What are three signs I'm emotionally off balance?

3. What can I do when I notice these signs?

Activity

The Importance of Scanning Your Body

Scanning your body helps you build awareness of physical sensations that are often linked to emotions, stress, or unresolved tension. This mindful check-in allows you to notice early signs of anxiety, fatigue, or overwhelm—signals your body sends before your mind catches up. Regular body scans can improve your connection to yourself, support emotional regulation, and serve as a grounding practice during moments of stress or recovery.

HOW TO: Body Scan Practice

Spend 5 minutes daily doing a mental body scan—from head to toe—and record physical or emotional sensations. This helps build awareness of your emotional warning signs before they escalate.

Body Scan Practice

Day	Physical Sensation	Emotional Sensation
Monday		
Tuesday		
Wednesday		
Thursday		
Friday		
Saturday		
Sunday		

What insight did you gain?

Coping Strategies and Healthy Alternatives

Coping Strategies and Healthy Alternatives

Responding to Triggers with Awareness, Not Automaticity

When we begin to recognize our emotional triggers and patterns, the next step is learning how to respond in ways that are constructive rather than reactive. This is where coping strategies and healthy alternatives come in. Coping strategies are the tools, practices, and intentional choices we use to manage emotional distress, soothe our nervous system, and create space for healing. They allow us to pause between a triggering event and our reaction, offering an opportunity to respond in alignment with our present values—not from old wounds or unconscious beliefs. Healthy alternatives don't erase triggers, but they give us more power and flexibility in how we handle them.

Triggers, whether internal (like thoughts, memories, or physical sensations) or external (such as people, places, or situations), can cause intense emotional reactions that feel overwhelming or even unsafe. Without awareness, these reactions often lead to patterns like shutting down, lashing out, using substances, people-pleasing, or dissociating. These responses may have once served a protective purpose, helping us survive painful or chaotic environments. However, over time, they can become automatic habits that reinforce harmful beliefs—such as "I'm not safe," "I'm not enough," or "I don't have control." Coping strategies help disrupt these patterns and offer new, more supportive ways to meet our emotional needs.

One of the most empowering aspects of using coping tools is the opportunity to rewire old beliefs and behaviors. **When you recognize a trigger and choose a healthy alternative instead of falling into an old pattern, you send yourself a new message—one that says, "I can handle this," or "My emotions are valid and manageable."** This begins to shift the core beliefs you've internalized over time. For example, if you typically withdraw when you feel overwhelmed, practicing grounding techniques or reaching out to a trusted friend can reinforce the belief that connection is safe and that you are worthy of support. If you tend to react with anger or control, practicing breathwork or self-reflection can help affirm the belief that you don't need to fight to be heard or seen.

Healthy alternatives come in many forms, and the key is choosing ones that resonate with your needs and values. Physical strategies might include taking a walk, stretching, dancing, or doing breathwork to release built-up tension. Mental and emotional strategies might include journaling, practicing mindfulness, challenging negative thoughts, or using affirmations that counter old beliefs. Relational strategies can involve seeking connection, setting boundaries, or talking with a supportive person. Creative outlets—like art, music, or writing—can also be powerful ways to express what you're feeling without judgment. The goal is not perfection, but consistency—using your tools often enough that they become more familiar than your old, reactive patterns.

Ultimately, the use of coping strategies and healthy alternatives helps you build emotional resilience and self-trust. **You begin to see that while you may not be able to control every trigger, you can control how you respond.** This shift creates space for healing. **You can acknowledge your past without being defined by it.** You can witness your triggers without becoming overwhelmed by them. And most importantly, you can begin to explore the roots of your beliefs with curiosity and compassion, knowing you now have tools to help you stay grounded and empowered in the process. In this way, coping is not just about "getting through"—it's about building a foundation for lasting emotional growth and transformation.

Self-Assessment

Coping Strategies and Healthy Alternatives

Instructions: Rate each statement on a scale from *1* (Strongly Disagree) to *5* (Strongly Agree).

1. I have a variety of healthy coping strategies I can use when I feel overwhelmed or triggered.
2. When I feel emotionally dysregulated, I know how to calm myself down in a safe and healthy way.
3. I can usually choose a helpful response rather than falling into old, automatic reactions.
4. I regularly practice coping tools (like deep breathing, journaling, movement, or setting boundaries) to support my emotional well-being.
5. I can tell the difference between helpful coping strategies and harmful or avoidant behaviors.
6. I respond to emotional discomfort by acknowledging it rather than suppressing, avoiding, or numbing it.
7. I am working to replace unhealthy coping habits with healthier alternatives.
8. I feel empowered and supported by the tools I use to care for my emotional health.

1 – Strongly Disagree	2 – Disagree	3 – Neutral /Unsure	4 – Agree	5 – Strongly Agree

Scoring Guide:

8–16: Limited use of healthy coping—consider building a toolbox of safe, intentional strategies.

17–28: Moderate coping awareness—some tools are working, but there's room for consistency or variety.

29–40: Strong coping foundation—you're likely using thoughtful strategies to navigate emotional challenges.

Worksheet: Coping Strategies and Healthy Alternatives

Instructions: For each statement below, circle the number that best reflects your current experience.

Scale: *1* = Strongly Disagree *2* = Disagree *3* = Neutral *4* = Agree *5* = Strongly Agree

1. I have a variety of healthy coping strategies I can use when I feel overwhelmed or triggered.

1 2 3 4 5

____

____

____

____

2. When I feel emotionally dysregulated, I know how to calm myself down in a safe and healthy way.

1 2 3 4 5

____

____

____

____

3. I can usually choose a helpful response rather than falling into old, automatic reactions.

1 2 3 4 5

____

____

____

____

4. I regularly practice coping tools (like deep breathing, journaling, movement, or setting boundaries).

1 2 3 4 5

____

____

5. I can tell the difference between helpful coping strategies and harmful or avoidant behaviors.
1 2 3 4 5

6. I respond to emotional discomfort by acknowledging it rather than suppressing, avoiding, or numbing it.
1 2 3 4 5

7. I am actively working to replace unhealthy coping habits with healthier alternatives.
1 2 3 4 5

8. I feel empowered and supported by the tools I use to care for my emotional health.
1 2 3 4 5

Reflection Activity:

1. Which coping strategies have worked well for you recently?

2. What unhelpful patterns or habits would you like to shift or release?

3. What is one healthy coping strategy you'd like to try or practice more often?

4. When do you most need your coping tools—and how can you remind yourself to use them in those moments?

Bonus Challenge: "Build Your Coping Menu"

List at least three healthy alternatives for times when you're feeling...

Anxious:

1.
2.
3.

Sad or low:

1. ______________________
2. ______________________
3. ______________________

Angry or frustrated:

1. ______________________
2. ______________________
3. ______________________

Journal

1. What coping tools have helped me in the past? Which ones haven't?

2. How do I feel after using a healthy coping skill versus a harmful one?

3. What new strategy do I want to try the next time I feel triggered?

Activity

The Importance of Having a Coping Skills Toolbox

Having a coping skills toolbox provides you with a ready set of healthy strategies to manage stress, regulate emotions, and navigate challenging situations. Just like a physical toolbox holds tools for different problems, your coping toolbox holds personalized techniques—like deep breathing, journaling, movement, or reaching out for support—that help you stay grounded and resilient. Building this toolkit increases your sense of control and supports long-term emotional wellness and recovery.

HOW TO: Build a Coping Skills Toolbox

A Coping Skills Toolbox is usually a figurative thing we use to "store" our learned coping skills. Some people need a visual. Problem solved!

Create a written or visual list (or a decorated box) of healthy coping strategies (deep breathing, texting a friend, walking, journaling, etc.). Keep it accessible and add to it over time.

Healthy Coping Strategies

1.
2.
3.
4.
5.
6.
7.
8.
9.
10.

Cameron

Personal Recovery Story

Before coming into recovery, I would spend hours searching for foil in highly populated homeless areas, which is how I would support my habit by finding tutors or paraphernalia with drugs left on it. When that failed, I would panhandle for maybe 10 to 20 dollars a day. On average, I was using 5-10 blues a day. I had gotten sepsis and was hospitalized for a month. Three chest tubes and a surgery on my lungs, and 2 weeks later, I relapsed. I cut myself off from any form of help and didn't feel like I was worthy of even asking for it. This made panhandling painfully difficult. I was in a codependent relationship where neither of us valued ourselves and prioritized the other's needs. This caused both our lives to spiral into suffering. Also, I primarily ate donuts out of a local donut shop’s dumpster, as well as any other discarded food.

I came into rehab because of how apparent it had become that I was a direct negative influence on the life of the only person who showed me they loved me in a way that registered. However, after regaining some self-esteem and confidence, I realized it was my fault that people felt that treating me as a doormat or a pushover was acceptable. I taught people how to treat me and got mad at them for it. Instead of setting boundaries, I expected them to recognize the way they were treating me was unfair and change it. By setting boundaries on others and not compromising my values for others, I have become more confident using my voice and understanding where I fit into the world. This is my third real attempt, but my first rehab and A.A. attempt.

I don't have a problem telling people “No” anymore, or struggle with talking about my emotions. However, I still struggle to recognize them. One of my core values is honesty, and I have found a job where I am accepted as I am. I recently got arrested for an old warrant and wasn't afraid of losing my job or angry at getting arrested. I was actually able to enjoy the time I spent being detained. One thing that has been instrumental in my recovery is finding a place where I belong and feel wholly accepted and becoming a part of it instead of maintaining my desire to be a background character in my own life. That place is A.A., but I have been blessed that my workplace is just as welcoming and accepting of me and my past.

If I feel like relapse is a good idea, that means I have retreated back into my shell and cut off all my outside support. Currently, I have no desire to escape anymore. I care about myself now and don't want to slowly or quickly kill myself. I have purpose and people who rely on me and who I can rely on, and it is a wonderful feeling. Living in sober living, I have a car, and I am financially stable. 11 months sober.

Final Thoughts

Recognizing and understanding your triggers is a vital step in uncovering the beliefs and behaviors that shape your emotional world. Whether they are internal or external, triggers often activate automatic reactions rooted in past experiences, especially those tied to trauma or unmet emotional needs. These reactions are not random—they are learned responses designed to protect you at one time in your life. By slowing down and identifying the moments you feel emotionally charged, you begin to uncover the early warning signs and emotional cues that signal something deeper is being stirred.

Through this process, you also begin to recognize the emotional and behavioral patterns that have repeated throughout your life. These patterns are tied to core beliefs—often negative ones—that have taken root over time. Beliefs such as "I'm not worthy," "I have to be perfect," or "My feelings don't matter" frequently operate beneath the surface and shape how you respond to stress, relationships, and challenges. Bringing awareness to these patterns empowers you to question, challenge, and begin to rewrite them.

Ultimately, healing begins when you replace unconscious reactions with conscious coping strategies and healthy alternatives. These tools help you regulate your nervous system, respond to triggers with clarity, and rebuild trust in yourself. As you continue to explore your triggers and patterns, you'll gain more insight into your identity, your needs, and your capacity for change. This chapter invites you to view your reactions not as flaws, but as doorways to self-understanding—where your past meets the power of your present awareness.

Reflection

1. **What types of situations tend to activate strong emotional reactions in me?**
   Explore recent or recurring moments where you felt overwhelmed, shut down, or reactive. What patterns do you notice?

2. **When I feel triggered, what do I typically do to cope—and how does that serve or hurt me?**
   Be honest, but gentle with yourself. Are you avoiding, numbing, yelling, or isolating? What's the need underneath?

3. **If my triggers could speak, what would they say they need from me?**
   Imagine your triggers are messengers. What might they be trying to protect or remind you of?

saturday

Creative Experiwence & Self-Discovery

Weekend Work

Exploring identity and emotions through art, music, or writing provides a creative outlet for expressing feelings that may be difficult to put into words. These forms of expression allow you to process experiences, release emotional pain, and gain insight into your inner world in a safe, nonverbal way. In recovery, creative activities can help you rediscover who you are beyond addiction, build confidence, and foster a sense of purpose and healing. They offer a meaningful way to explore your story, express your truth, and connect with others on a deeper level.

Goal:

Explore identity and emotions through art, music, or writing.

Activities:

- Vision board creation
- Guided art therapy workshop
- Music circle or drumming session
- Poetry journaling or storytelling circle

10 Creative Expression Activities I would Like to Try:
•
•
•
•
•
•
•
•
•
•

Monday

Process, Recharge, Reset, and Reflect

The Importance of Rest: To Process, Recharge, Reset, and Reflect- Part 2

Recharging is not just physical—it is emotional, mental, and spiritual as well. Just like a phone loses power after constant use, so do we. Taking intentional rest allows us to fill our emotional tank, reconnect with joy, and restore balance. It's in the pause that we regain strength to keep going—not out of obligation, but from a place of wholeness.

Resetting is an act of choice. **Life can become mechanical when we're stuck in survival mode or routine.** Rest gives us the opportunity to interrupt that cycle and return to the center. It's a way to ask ourselves, "Is this still working for me?" or "What needs to shift?" Whether we realize it or not, rest gives us a reset button—a fresh perspective that often brings new ideas, solutions, and insights.

3

Developing emotional awareness & regulation

Introduction

Developing emotional awareness and regulation is a foundational skill for personal growth and well-being. It begins with the ability to identify and name emotions accurately, which helps us make sense of what we're feeling and why. Recognizing how emotions show up in the body—tight muscles, racing heart, fatigue—strengthens our understanding of the mind-body connection and provides early cues to emotional shifts. By becoming more aware of our emotional triggers—specific situations, thoughts, or memories that spark intense reactions—we create space for insight rather than impulsivity. This awareness allows us to track patterns and make more intentional choices.

Emotional regulation involves learning how to respond rather than react. **While reactions are often immediate and driven by emotion, responses are thoughtful and grounded in awareness.** Building an emotional regulation toolbox—filled with techniques like deep breathing, grounding exercises, journaling, physical movement, and reaching out for support—gives us healthy alternatives to manage overwhelming emotions. As we strengthen these skills, we increase resilience, improve our relationships, and create more balance in our daily lives.

Objective

The objective of this section is to help individuals build skills in emotional awareness and regulation by learning to identify and name emotions, understand the connection between thoughts, feelings, and physical sensations, recognize personal emotional triggers, and develop a personalized emotional regulation toolbox. Participants will explore the difference between reacting and responding, with the goal of cultivating greater self-control, emotional balance, and healthier interpersonal relationships.

W3: Agenda

M	Identifying and Naming Emotions
T	Understanding the Mind-Body Connection
W	Recognizing Emotional Triggers
T	Building an Emotional Regulation Toolbox
F	Responding VS. Reacting
S	Sober Socializing & Connection Building

Monday

Identifying and Naming Emotions

Identifying and Naming Emotions Through Types of Triggers

A Path to Emotional Awareness and Regulation

Emotions are a central part of the human experience, influencing how we think, act, and relate to others. Yet many people go through life without truly understanding what they feel or why. Emotional awareness—the ability to identify, name, and make sense of our feelings—is a crucial first step in emotional regulation. **Learning to accurately identify emotions can help us navigate stress, improve relationships, and make healthier decisions.** One powerful way to develop emotional awareness is through exploring our emotional triggers. Triggers are external events or internal experiences that provoke strong emotional reactions. By identifying the types of triggers we encounter and naming the emotions they evoke, we begin to uncover patterns, beliefs, and unmet needs that influence our behavior.

There are many types of emotional triggers. They can be situational, such as conflict, criticism, or rejection; relational, such as abandonment or betrayal; or internal, such as self-doubt, shame, or feeling unworthy. Triggers often originate from past experiences, particularly those involving trauma, unmet needs, or core beliefs formed in childhood. For example, someone who was frequently ignored as a child may feel disproportionately hurt when they are left out of a social gathering as an adult. The emotional intensity of the moment may seem confusing until we connect it to a deeper wound or belief—like "I'm not important" or "I don't belong." Naming the emotion in that moment—perhaps sadness, shame, or loneliness—gives clarity to what's happening internally and creates an opportunity to respond with intention rather than react from old patterns.

The process of naming emotions may sound simple, but it requires practice and patience. Many people grow up in environments where emotions were dismissed, punished, or simply never talked about. As a result, they may only have access to vague labels like "good" or "bad," or rely on secondary emotions like anger, while the primary feelings of fear, hurt, or sadness go unrecognized. Building an emotional vocabulary allows us to fine-tune our self-awareness and better communicate with others. Saying "I feel overwhelmed and anxious" carries more insight and possibility for action than simply saying "I'm stressed." This level of clarity opens the door to understanding why a trigger affected us and how we can manage it moving forward.

Triggers often shine a light on our deeper emotional wounds and belief systems. When we feel triggered, it's an invitation to reflect: *What belief is being activated? What past experience does this remind me of?* In this way, identifying and naming emotions in the context of our triggers becomes a tool for self-discovery. It helps us trace our current emotional responses back to early messages we received about ourselves and the world. For instance, if someone feels anxious every time they make a mistake, it might reflect a core belief like "I have to be perfect to be accepted." That belief likely stems from past environments where mistakes were harshly criticized or led to emotional withdrawal from caregivers. By acknowledging and naming the emotions—fear, shame, pressure—we can begin to rewrite the old narrative and make room for self-compassion and healing.

Furthermore, naming emotions helps us regulate them. **Neuroscience research shows that simply labeling a feeling reduces activity in the amygdala—the brain's fear center—and activates the prefrontal cortex, which is responsible for reasoning and decision-making.** This means that when we name our emotions, we are literally calming our brains and increasing our ability to choose a measured response. This process turns reactivity into mindfulness. Instead of yelling when we feel disrespected or shutting down when we feel vulnerable, we can pause, name what we're feeling, and choose how we want to respond. Over time, this strengthens our emotional regulation muscles and builds resilience.

Identifying and naming emotions also enhances our relationships. **When we can clearly express what we feel, others are more likely to respond with empathy and understanding.** It reduces the chance of miscommunication or escalating conflict. For example, saying "I felt hurt and left out when I wasn't invited" is more effective than lashing out or withdrawing. It creates space for honest conversations and emotional repair. It also models emotional intelligence for others, contributing to more connected and emotionally healthy relationships.

Developing emotional awareness and regulation through identifying triggers and naming emotions is a skill that takes time, practice, and self-compassion. It requires slowing down, tuning in, and getting curious about our inner world. Journaling, body scans, and using feelings wheels or emotion charts can be helpful tools in this process. Working with a therapist or in a group setting can also provide support and feedback as we build emotional fluency. **The more we practice, the more we begin to trust our emotions as messengers rather than threats.** We become less reactive and more rooted in who we are and what we need.

In conclusion, learning to identify and name emotions in response to triggers is a powerful way to build emotional awareness and regulation. It allows us to recognize old belief systems, understand the origins of our emotional reactions, and make conscious choices rather than operate on autopilot. **By engaging with our emotions instead of avoiding them, we foster personal growth, healthier relationships, and a more authentic connection to ourselves.** This work lays the foundation for lasting change and deeper emotional freedom.

Self-Assessment

Identifying and Naming Emotions

Instructions: Rate each statement on a scale from *1* (Strongly Disagree) to *5* (Strongly Agree).

1. I am able to recognize when I am feeling a strong emotion, even if I don't know exactly what it is.
2. I can accurately name the emotions I am experiencing (e.g., sad, anxious, frustrated, excited).
3. I notice changes in my body that help me identify what I am feeling (e.g., tension, energy, heat, heaviness).
4. I can distinguish between similar emotions like anger and disappointment, or anxiety and excitement.
5. I reflect on what triggered my emotional response and try to understand why I felt that way.
6. I feel comfortable expressing my emotions using specific words rather than vague terms like "fine" or "bad."
7. I am aware when I am feeling more than one emotion at the same time and can name each one.
8. I use tools like journaling, talking, or visual aids (e.g., emotion wheels) to help identify how I feel.

1 – Strongly Disagree	2 – Disagree	3 – Neutral /Unsure	4 – Agree	5 – Strongly Agree

Scoring Guide:

8–16: Low awareness – Emotional identification may be limited or unclear; support and practice needed to build foundational skills.

17–28: Moderate awareness – Some ability to identify and name emotions, though further development could increase clarity and confidence.

29–40: High awareness – Strong ability to identify, name, and reflect on emotions; demonstrates emotional insight and self-awareness.

Worksheet: Identifying and Naming Emotions

Instructions:
Read each statement below and reflect on how much it applies to you. Use the space provided to write your thoughts, give examples, or note any patterns you notice in your emotional experiences.

1. I am able to recognize when I am feeling a strong emotion, even if I don't know exactly what it is.

   What does that feel like in your body? What are some recent examples?

   ____
   ____
   ____
   ____

2. I can accurately name the emotions I am experiencing (e.g., sad, anxious, frustrated, excited).
   Which emotions are easiest to identify? Which is harder?

   ____
   ____
   ____
   ____

3. I notice changes in my body that help me identify what I am feeling (e.g., tension, energy, heat, heaviness).
   What physical signs help you recognize different emotions?

   ____
   ____
   ____
   ____

4. I can distinguish between similar emotions like anger and disappointment or anxiety and excitement.
How do you tell them apart? Are there situations where they overlap?

---

5. I reflect on what triggered my emotional response and try to understand why I felt that way.
When was the last time you did this? What did you discover about yourself?

---

6. I feel comfortable expressing my emotions using specific words rather than vague terms like "fine" or "bad."
What words do you typically use to describe your emotions?

---

7. I am aware when I am feeling more than one emotion at the same time and can name each one.
How do you process or express mixed emotions?

---

8. I use tools like journaling, talking, or visual aids (e.g., emotion wheels) to help identify how I feel.
Which tools do you use, or which would you like to try?

Journal

1. What emotion did I feel the strongest today? Describe the situation and how you knew.

2. Are there any emotions I avoid or struggle to name? Why might that be?

3. How do I usually express emotions like anger, sadness, or joy?

Activity

The Importance of Recognizing Emotions

Recognizing your emotions is essential for understanding how you respond to situations and for managing your mental health effectively. When you can identify what you're feeling, you gain insight into your needs and triggers, which helps you communicate more clearly and make healthier choices. This awareness is the foundation for emotional regulation, deeper self-understanding, and building stronger relationships.

HOW TO: Emotions Wheel

Use the Feelings Wheel on the next page to circle or highlight three emotions you experienced today. Reflect on when and why they occurred.

The Feelings Wheel

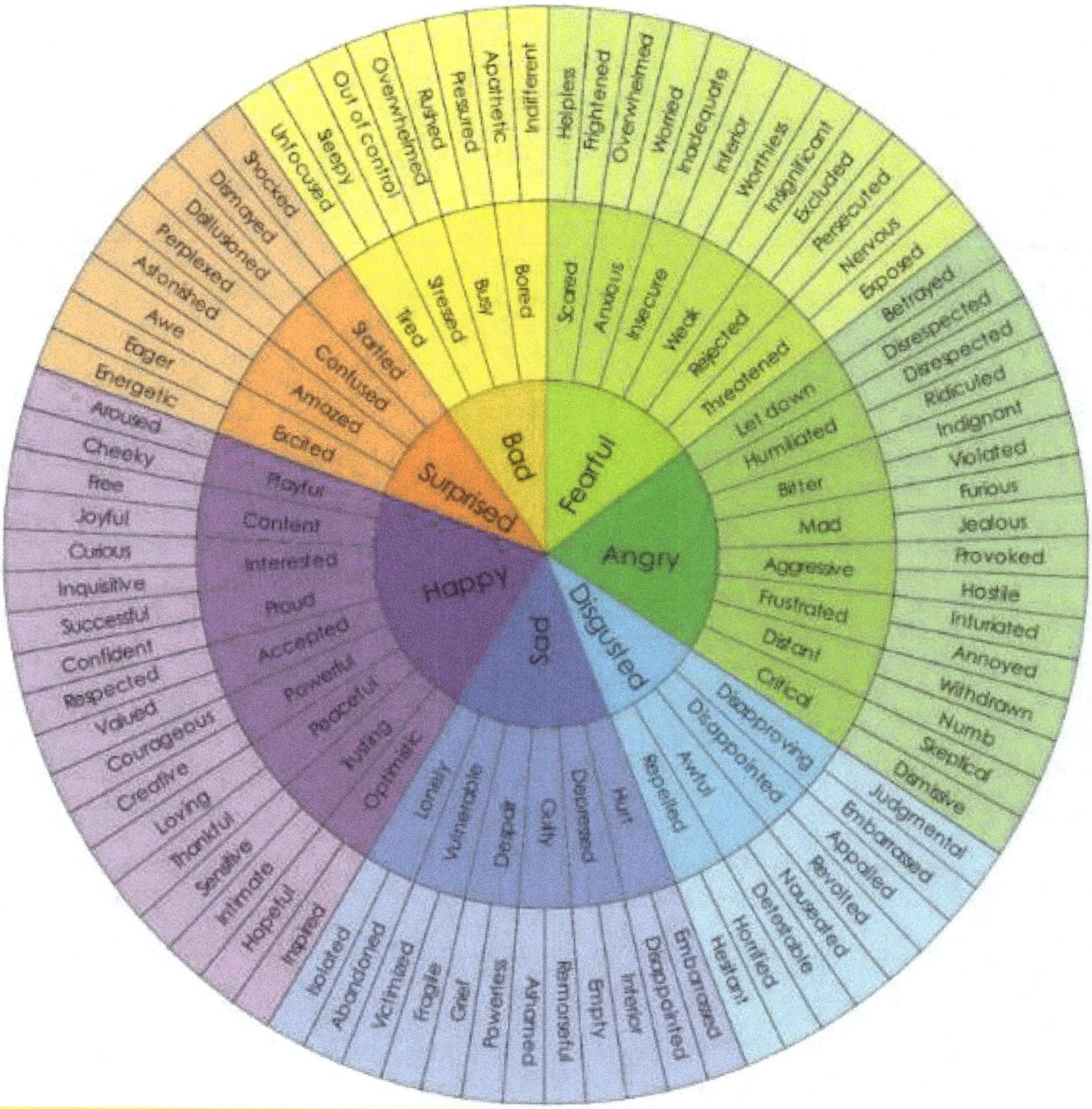

Developed by Dr. Gloria Wilcox

Reflection Activity:

3 emotions you experienced today	When and why did these emotions occur

Judi

Personal Recovery Story

I destroyed my entire life in less than five years. I became addicted to fentanyl at *38* years old, and by the time I turned *40*, I was spending my birthday in treatment. I went through four different treatment programs, each time hoping this would be the one that stuck—but I always relapsed within a week or two. After my fourth attempt, I relapsed again. But this time felt different. I was emotionally drained, physically broken, and completely exhausted by the cycle I was trapped in. Out of desperation, I called a local outpatient recovery center that offered Medication-Assisted Treatment (MAT), and they got me in right away. That phone call saved my life.

With MAT, weekly group therapy, monthly individual sessions, and a daily schedule packed so full I barely had time to think about using, I finally started to build a real foundation in recovery. I stayed on MAT for *2½* years, and when it was time, I began a slow *14*-month taper off the medication. It was tough, but I was ready. When I finally took my last dose, I felt truly free for the first time in years. My clean date is *11/18/2021*, and this November, I'll celebrate four years clean from fentanyl. Recovery didn't come easy or fast, but it came—and every day I wake up sober is a day I'm grateful to be alive.

tuesday

Understanding the Mind-Body Connection

Understanding the Mind-Body Connection Through Types of Triggers

A Path to Emotional Awareness and Regulation

The mind and body are deeply interconnected, continuously influencing one another in ways that shape how we think, feel, and respond to life. The mind-body connection refers to the dynamic relationship between our thoughts, emotions, and physical sensations. It plays a critical role in emotional awareness and regulation. **When we experience emotional triggers—whether from external situations or internal memories—the body often reacts before the mind fully registers what is happening.** By tuning into these physical cues, we gain valuable insight into our emotional states and begin to uncover deeper beliefs that influence our behavior. Understanding this connection is essential for healing emotional wounds, regulating overwhelming feelings, and making conscious, empowered choices.

Emotional triggers activate physiological responses in the body. These can include rapid heartbeat, shallow breathing, muscle tension, nausea, fatigue, or even numbness. These sensations are often part of the body's automatic stress response, sometimes called the "fight, flight, freeze, or fawn" reaction. For example, if someone feels triggered by perceived criticism, their body might tense up, their stomach might twist, or they might feel flushed or shaky. These reactions are not random—they are the body's way of signaling perceived danger based on past experiences. In many cases, these responses are tied to deeply rooted beliefs, such as "I'm not good enough," "I'm unsafe," or "I must be perfect to be loved." These beliefs, often formed in early life, shape how we interpret present-day situations and influence how our body responds to emotional stimuli.

Understanding these physical reactions as emotional messengers allows us to shift from reactivity to regulation. **Rather than suppressing or ignoring bodily sensations, we can learn to interpret them as cues to pause, check in, and ask ourselves what we are feeling and why.** For example, a tight chest and clenched jaw might signal anger or fear, prompting us to reflect on what triggered those feelings. Was it a sense of being disrespected? A reminder of a past betrayal? These sensations offer a direct path to understanding our internal world. By learning to "listen" to the body, we deepen our emotional awareness and begin to connect present-day experiences to long-held emotional patterns and beliefs.

There are many types of triggers that activate the mind-body connection. External triggers might include conflict, rejection, loud noises, or certain environments. Internal triggers may include thoughts, memories, or physiological states like hunger or fatigue. Some triggers are subtle and layered, such as feeling anxious in a group setting without immediately understanding why. Upon closer examination, it may connect to past experiences of exclusion, ridicule, or feeling invisible. In these moments, the body is often the first to alert us that something is wrong—through a racing heart, dizziness, or a sudden drop in energy. Recognizing these patterns helps us map the relationship between triggers, emotional responses, and bodily sensations, offering a powerful tool for healing and self-awareness.

By exploring the mind-body connection, we also come to understand how trauma and chronic stress affect emotional regulation. Unresolved trauma often lives in the body, leading to heightened sensitivity to triggers and difficulty managing emotions. **Individuals who have experienced trauma may live in a constant state of hyperarousal or dissociation, where the body is either in a state of alertness or shutdown.** Learning to recognize these physiological states as responses to emotional triggers can be a turning point in recovery. It allows us to approach our reactions with curiosity and compassion rather than shame or self-judgment. Over time, we can learn to calm the nervous system through grounding practices, breathwork, movement, and mindfulness, all of which help restore balance and a sense of safety.

Practicing body awareness is a key step in strengthening the mind-body connection. Techniques like body scanning, mindful breathing, progressive muscle relaxation, and somatic tracking can help individuals become more attuned to the signals their body sends. Journaling about physical sensations during emotional moments can also increase awareness and provide insight into hidden emotional patterns. For instance, noticing that a particular person or situation always brings tightness in the chest might prompt reflection on underlying beliefs or unresolved wounds related to that dynamic. These practices create space to notice, name, and nurture the emotional experience rather than being controlled by it.

Ultimately, developing awareness of the mind-body connection empowers individuals to respond rather than react to emotional triggers. Instead of being overwhelmed by intense feelings, we can recognize the early warning signs in our body, name the emotions, trace them to their roots, and apply healthy regulation strategies. This kind of self-awareness is not just about managing emotions—it's about healing the emotional wounds beneath them. It is about challenging and rewriting the core beliefs that keep us stuck in cycles of fear, shame, or self-protection.

In conclusion, understanding the mind-body connection through emotional triggers is a transformative step in developing emotional awareness and regulation. It helps us become attuned to the ways our body reflects our emotional world and provides a gateway into deeper self-knowledge and healing. As we learn to interpret the language of the body, we begin to uncover the roots of our beliefs, rewrite old narratives, and build a foundation of emotional safety and strength. **This integration of mind and body not only fosters personal growth but also enhances our ability to connect, trust, and thrive in our relationships and daily life.**

Self-Assessment

Self-Assessment: Understanding the Mind-Body Connection

Instructions: Rate each statement on a scale from *1* (Strongly Disagree) to *5* (Strongly Agree).

1. I notice when my body changes in response to stress or strong emotions (e.g., tense muscles, racing heart, fatigue).
2. I pay attention to physical sensations as signals of my emotional state.
3. I can tell when I'm emotionally overwhelmed by tuning into how my body feels.
4. I understand that my emotions can influence my physical health and energy levels.
5. I use body-based techniques (e.g., breathing, stretching, grounding) to help calm my emotions.
6. I am able to identify emotional triggers by noticing the physical reactions they create in me.
7. I recognize how unresolved emotions can stay stored in the body and impact how I feel physically.
8. I try to bring awareness to both my thoughts and my body when I feel emotionally activated.

1 – Strongly Disagree	2 – Disagree	3 – Neutral /Unsure	4 – Agree	5 – Strongly Agree

Scoring Guide:

8–16: Limited connection – May benefit from learning how emotions show up physically and using body-based awareness tools.

17–28: Moderate connection – Some awareness of how emotions and the body interact; practice can deepen this understanding.

29–40: Strong connection – Highly attuned to the mind-body relationship; likely to regulate emotions through physical awareness and tools.

Worksheet: Exploring the Mind-Body Connection

Instructions:
Reflect on each statement below. Use the space provided to describe your experiences, give examples, or explore how you relate to each idea. There are no right or wrong answers—this is about building self-awareness.

1. **I notice when my body changes in response to stress or strong emotions.**
   What physical signs (e.g., tension, heart rate, stomach discomfort) do you notice when you feel overwhelmed or upset?

   ____
   ____
   ____
   ____

2. **I pay attention to physical sensations as signals of my emotional state.**
   How does your body help you understand your feelings before your mind catches up?

   ____
   ____
   ____
   ____

3. **I can tell when I'm emotionally overwhelmed by tuning into how my body feels.**
   What does emotional overload feel like in your body? What are your early warning signs?

   ____
   ____
   ____
   ____

4. **I understand that my emotions can influence my physical health and energy levels.**
Have you noticed patterns (e.g., fatigue, headaches, tension) tied to stress, sadness, or anxiety? Describe them.

___
___
___
___

5. **I use body-based techniques (like breathing, stretching, or grounding) to calm myself when I'm emotional.**
Which techniques work for you? Which ones would you like to try more often?

___
___
___
___

6. **I identify emotional triggers by noticing the physical reactions they create.**
What recent situation triggered a physical response in your body? What emotion did you connect it to?

___
___
___
___

7. **I recognize how unresolved emotions might be stored in the body.**
Have you ever felt physical discomfort that seemed connected to emotional pain or stress? What was that like?

___
___
___
___

8. **I bring awareness to both my thoughts and body when emotionally activated.** What helps you stay present and connected to your body during intense emotions?

Bonus Reflection Questions:

- Which responses helped you learn something new about yourself?
- What would help you deepen your mind-body awareness?
- What's one small step you can take this week to connect more with your body when emotions rise?

Journal

1. **Where in my body do I notice emotions the most?**

2. **How does my body feel when I'm at peace?**

3. **What physical signs could alert me that I'm feeling overwhelmed?**

Activity

The Importance of Body Scanning and the Mind-Body Connection

Body scanning strengthens the mind-body connection by helping you tune into physical sensations that reflect your emotional and mental states. Tension, discomfort, or pain often carries messages from your inner world, signaling stress, anxiety, or unresolved feelings. By regularly checking in with your body, you learn to interpret these signals with curiosity and care, deepening your self-awareness and supporting emotional regulation, healing, and holistic well-being.

HOW TO: 3-Minute Body Scan

Do a 3-minute body scan. Slowly notice each area of your body. Write down where you feel tension or ease. Label any emotions that come up.

Body Scan Practice

Day	Feel Tension	Feel Ease
Monday		
Tuesday		
Wednesday		
Thursday		
Friday		
Saturday		
Sunday		

What insight did you gain?

Wednesday

Recognizing Emotional Triggers

Recognizing Emotional Triggers Through Types of Triggers: A Foundation for Emotional Awareness and Regulation

Emotional triggers are powerful indicators of our inner world. They are emotional responses that are often intense, sudden, and disproportionate to the situation at hand. These triggers, whether sparked by specific situations, words, tones, or even memories, are rooted in our past experiences and the beliefs we carry about ourselves, others, and the world. Recognizing emotional triggers is an essential part of developing emotional awareness and regulation. **When we become aware of what triggers us, why it happens, and how our body and mind respond, we begin to unlock the origins of our emotional patterns.** This process is not only a path to healing and growth but also a doorway to reshaping deeply held beliefs that may no longer serve us.

There are different types of emotional triggers, each connected to specific emotional needs, memories, or core beliefs. Some common categories of triggers include rejection, abandonment, criticism, failure, feeling disrespected, being ignored, or losing control. For instance, someone who was frequently dismissed or neglected during childhood might feel triggered when their ideas are overlooked in a group setting. Another person might have been shamed for showing vulnerability and now feels deeply uncomfortable or angry when they begin to feel emotionally exposed. These reactions often happen quickly and may not seem rational at the surface. But when explored further, they reveal important information about the past and about the beliefs that have shaped how we respond to the present.

Emotional triggers are not simply negative reactions—they are messages. They are the nervous system's way of alerting us to something that feels unsafe or unresolved. By learning to recognize and reflect on these reactions instead of avoiding or numbing them, we can begin to understand what they're trying to tell us. For example, if someone notices they feel a wave of anxiety every time they are asked to speak in public, that trigger might be linked to a fear of judgment, a past experience of embarrassment, or a belief that their voice doesn't matter. Recognizing that this anxiety isn't just about the current moment but is deeply connected to a belief or memory opens up the opportunity for healing and reframing.

Recognizing emotional triggers also helps us distinguish between the past and the present. **Many emotional responses are not just reactions to what is happening now—they are reactions to what *used* to happen.** When a situation reminds us, consciously or unconsciously, of a past wound, our nervous system responds as though the past is happening all over again. This is why some reactions feel so overwhelming. They're not just about today's event—they're layered with past pain and meaning. Bringing awareness to these moments helps us pause and say, "This feels familiar—where is this really coming from?" In that pause, we create a space between feeling and action, between trigger and reaction.

The goal of recognizing triggers is not to eliminate them altogether. Rather, it's to become more conscious of them so we can respond in healthier, more grounded ways. Emotional regulation begins when we can notice that we've been triggered, identify what we're feeling, and make choices about how to handle the situation. This might involve using grounding techniques, taking a break, practicing breathwork, journaling, or reaching out to someone for support. Over time, this practice helps build emotional resilience. We become more aware, more intentional, and more in control of our responses—even when emotions are strong.

This process of identifying triggers and regulating our responses also helps us explore the roots of our beliefs. **Every emotional trigger is connected to a story we've told ourselves—often without realizing it.** These stories might include: "I'm not worthy," "I always mess up," "People can't be trusted," or "I have to be perfect to be loved." These core beliefs develop from early life experiences, especially in our families, schools, or peer groups. **By bringing awareness to how a trigger activates these beliefs, we can begin to challenge them.** We can ask, "Is this belief still true for me? Does it help me, or hold me back?" As we question these beliefs, we create space to rewrite the inner narrative and replace it with one rooted in truth, self-compassion, and growth.

Recognizing emotional triggers also enhances our relationships. **When we understand our own triggers, we can communicate more clearly and assertively.** We can take responsibility for our reactions and share our needs without blame or defensiveness. We're also better able to hold space for others, recognizing that their reactions may be rooted in their own triggers and beliefs. This level of emotional intelligence fosters empathy, respect, and deeper connection in relationships of all kinds.

In conclusion, recognizing emotional triggers through the lens of emotional awareness and regulation is a transformative practice. It helps us shift from automatic reactions to conscious responses, from confusion to clarity, and from fear to empowerment. By understanding what sets off our emotional responses, we gain insight into the beliefs and experiences that shaped us—and begin the work of healing and growth. This self-awareness allows us to take ownership of our emotions, communicate more effectively, and create more meaningful, balanced relationships. **Ultimately, our triggers become guides, pointing us toward the areas within ourselves that are ready to be seen, healed, and transformed.**

Self-Assessment

Recognizing Emotional Triggers

Instructions: Rate each statement on a scale from *1* (Strongly Disagree) to *5* (Strongly Agree).

1. I can identify when a situation or person is triggering a strong emotional reaction in me.
2. I am aware of specific events or behaviors that tend to provoke intense feelings.
3. I notice physical changes in my body when I am emotionally triggered (e.g., heart racing, stomach tightness).
4. I can recognize the difference between my current emotional reaction and past experiences that influence it.
5. I understand how certain triggers relate to my past beliefs or experiences.
6. When triggered, I can pause to reflect on what is causing my reaction before responding.
7. I am able to name the emotions that come up when I am triggered.
8. I use my awareness of triggers to better manage my emotional responses.

1 – Strongly Disagree	2 – Disagree	3 – Neutral /Unsure	4 – Agree	5 – Strongly Agree

Interpretation of Total Score

Score Range	Awareness Level	Description
8 – 16	Emerging Awareness	You may benefit from practicing to better recognize and reflect on your emotional triggers.
17 – 28	Developing Awareness	You have some understanding of your emotional triggers and are working on managing them.
29 – 40	Strong Awareness	You are highly aware of your emotional triggers and are effectively managing your emotional responses.

Worksheet: Recognizing Emotional Triggers

Instructions:
Read each statement below and reflect on how much it applies to you. Use the space to write your thoughts, examples, or any patterns you notice.

1. I can identify when a situation or person is triggering a strong emotional reaction in me.
   What kinds of situations or people tend to trigger you?

   ____
   ____
   ____
   ____

2. I am aware of specific events or behaviors that tend to provoke intense feelings.
   Can you describe recent examples?

   ____
   ____
   ____
   ____

3. I notice physical changes in my body when I am emotionally triggered (e.g., heart racing, stomach tightness).
   What physical sensations do you experience when triggered?

   ____
   ____
   ____
   ____

4. I can recognize the difference between my current emotional reaction and past experiences that influence it.
   How do you tell the difference?

   ____
   ____
   ____
   ____

5. I understand how certain triggers relate to my past beliefs or experiences.
   Are there beliefs or past experiences connected to your triggers?

   ____
   ____
   ____
   ____

6. When triggered, I can pause to reflect on what is causing my reaction before responding.
   What helps you pause and reflect?

   ____
   ____
   ____
   ____

7. I am able to name the emotions that come up when I am triggered.
   Which emotions come up most often?

   ____
   ____
   ____
   ____

8. I use my awareness of triggers to better manage my emotional responses. *What strategies do you use to manage your reactions?*

Journal

1. **What triggered a strong emotion in me recently?**

2. **What patterns do I notice in my emotional triggers?**

3. **How do my past experiences influence my emotional reactions?**

Activity

The Importance of Recognizing Emotional Triggers

Recognizing emotional triggers helps you understand what situations, words, or experiences spark intense emotional reactions. These triggers often stem from past wounds or unmet needs and can lead to automatic responses like anger, withdrawal, or anxiety. By identifying them, you create space to pause, reflect, and respond more intentionally—turning reactive moments into opportunities for growth, healing, and self-compassion.

HOW TO: Trigger Tracker

Use a weekly chart to record situations, emotions felt, intensity level, and triggers. Review patterns at the end of the week.

Emotional Trigger Tracker

Day	Situation	Emotions Felt	Intensity Level (1-10)	Triggers
Monday				
Tuesday				
Wednesday				
Thursday				
Friday				
Saturday				
Sunday				

What insight did you gain?

____

____

____

____

thursday

Building an Emotional Regulation Toolbox

Building an Emotional Regulation Toolbox Through Types of Triggers

A Strategy for Awareness, Healing, and Growth

Emotional regulation is the ability to manage and respond to emotional experiences in ways that are constructive, rather than reactive or harmful. It involves staying aware of our emotions, understanding their origins, and using healthy tools to process or redirect emotional energy. One of the most effective ways to support this skill is by building an emotional regulation toolbox—a personalized set of practices, strategies, and resources we can turn to when we're emotionally triggered. This toolbox becomes especially important when navigating emotional triggers, which often arise from deep-seated beliefs and past experiences. **By learning to manage our triggers with effective tools, we create space to heal, grow, and respond to life with intention and self-compassion.**

Triggers can come in many forms, and each type may call for a different regulation strategy. Some common types of emotional triggers include perceived rejection, failure, disrespect, abandonment, or even sensory experiences that remind us of past trauma. For example, a loud voice might instantly cause someone to freeze or shut down, not because of the current moment alone, but because it mirrors past experiences of yelling and emotional abuse. **When we're not prepared to recognize and manage these triggers, we may fall into automatic patterns of reaction—shouting back, withdrawing, using substances, or self-sabotaging.** But when we build a regulation toolbox, we have concrete ways to ground ourselves, gain perspective, and engage in healthier behaviors.

The first step in building this toolbox is understanding the types of triggers that affect us most. This requires self-reflection and awareness. By noticing patterns—what situations evoke strong emotional reactions, what physical sensations accompany them, and what thoughts or beliefs are activated—we can begin to identify our unique triggers. For example, if someone becomes overwhelmed with anxiety every time they are given constructive criticism, they might trace that reaction back to a belief like "I'm never good enough" or "Mistakes mean I'll be rejected." Knowing this pattern helps determine which tools will be most helpful when the trigger is activated. It also allows us to work on the underlying belief that fuels the emotional response.

An emotional regulation toolbox should be diverse, with strategies that support the body, mind, and emotions. For the body, tools might include deep breathing, grounding exercises, stretching, walking, or cold water exposure. These techniques help soothe the nervous system and bring us back into the present moment. **When we're triggered, our body often reacts with increased heart rate, shallow breathing, muscle tension, or a sense of numbness.** Using a body-based tool can quickly regulate these responses and prevent further emotional escalation.

For the mind, cognitive tools such as reframing thoughts, using affirmations, practicing mindfulness, or journaling can be powerful. These tools help us make sense of what's happening and challenge distorted thinking. For example, if a trigger causes a flood of thoughts like "I'm a failure" or "They hate me," using a thought journal to examine the evidence and reframe the belief can provide relief and clarity. This process supports the deeper work of exploring and reshaping core beliefs that have been formed over time—often from childhood environments or early life relationships.

Emotion-focused tools are also vital. These include creative expression (such as art, music, or writing), emotional check-ins, talking to a supportive friend, or allowing oneself to cry or express feelings in a safe way. These tools give permission for the emotion to be felt and honored rather than pushed away or judged. **When we're triggered, it's not always about "fixing" the feeling, but rather creating space to process it without shame.** Over time, these emotional tools help us become more attuned to what we need in moments of distress and more compassionate toward our emotional experience.

Incorporating proactive regulation strategies into daily routines can also increase our emotional resilience. Things like regular movement, healthy sleep, balanced nutrition, creative hobbies, and time in nature strengthen our baseline regulation and make us less susceptible to being overwhelmed by triggers. A well-stocked toolbox isn't just about reacting in the moment—it's also about preparing and strengthening ourselves for emotional challenges before they arise.

Importantly, using regulation tools helps us interrupt old patterns and become more intentional in how we relate to others and ourselves. When a trigger once led to self-doubt or rage, using a regulation strategy can create a new outcome. This shift supports a re-patterning of belief systems. Each time we choose a healthy tool over an impulsive reaction, we reinforce a new narrative: "I am capable of handling this," "I am safe now," or "I have the power to choose my response." This gradual rewriting of beliefs can lead to profound emotional healing and growth.

In conclusion, building an emotional regulation toolbox is a foundational practice for managing emotional triggers, increasing self-awareness, and supporting long-term emotional health. It equips us to face the moments that once overwhelmed us and transforms them into opportunities for reflection and growth. By learning to understand our triggers and use tailored regulation strategies, we not only improve our emotional responses—we also uncover and challenge the beliefs beneath them. This work allows us to show up in our lives with more authenticity, stability, and self-trust. Ultimately, emotional regulation is not just about calming down—it's about reclaiming our ability to respond with clarity, purpose, and compassion.

Self-Assessment

Building an Emotional Regulation Toolbox

Instructions: Rate each statement on a scale from *1* (Strongly Disagree) to *5* (Strongly Agree).

1. I have specific strategies I use to calm myself when I feel overwhelmed.
2. I am aware of different tools (e.g., breathing exercises, grounding, journaling) that help regulate my emotions.
3. I regularly practice emotional regulation techniques to strengthen my ability to manage stress.
4. When I feel triggered, I can choose a tool from my emotional regulation toolbox to help me cope.
5. I have learned which regulation strategies work best for me in different emotional situations.
6. I feel confident using body-based techniques (like deep breathing or stretching) to calm my emotions.
7. I use creative outlets (such as art, music, or writing) to help process difficult emotions.
8. I continue to add new tools and strategies to my emotional regulation toolbox.

1 – Strongly Disagree	2 – Disagree	3 – Neutral /Unsure	4 – Agree	5 – Strongly Agree

Scoring Guide:

8–16: Beginning to build – You are starting to develop emotional regulation skills and tools.

17–28: Developing – You have a growing toolbox and use some strategies regularly.

29–40: Strong – You have a well-established toolbox and use a variety of effective strategies to regulate emotions.

Worksheet: Building an Emotional Regulation Toolbox

Instructions:

Reflect on each statement below. Use the space to explore your current strategies, areas for growth, or examples from your life. There are no right or wrong answers—this is for your self-awareness and growth.

1. I have specific strategies I use to calm myself when I feel overwhelmed. *What are they? How often do you use them?*

____

____

____

____

2. I am aware of different tools (e.g., breathing exercises, grounding, journaling) that help regulate my emotions.
Which tools do you know about? Which ones have you tried?

____

____

____

____

3. I regularly practice emotional regulation techniques to strengthen my ability to manage stress.
What do you practice consistently? What helps you stay grounded during tough moments?

____

____

____

____

4. When I feel triggered, I can choose a tool from my emotional regulation toolbox to help me cope.
What's your "go-to" tool in stressful moments? Does it usually help?

____
____
____
____

5. I have learned which regulation strategies work best for me in different emotional situations.
Which tools work best when you're anxious? Sad? Angry? Overstimulated?

____
____
____
____

6. I feel confident using body-based techniques (like deep breathing or stretching) to calm my emotions.
Which body-based tools help you most? Do you practice them regularly?

____
____
____
____

7. I use creative outlets (such as art, music, or writing) to help process difficult emotions.
What creative outlets bring you emotional relief or clarity?

____
____
____
____

8. I continue to add new tools and strategies to my emotional regulation toolbox. *What new strategies would you like to try or learn more about?*

Self-Assessment

1. What has helped me calm down or feel more grounded in the past?

2. What regulation tools do I want to try?

3. How do I know when I need to use a regulation strategy?

Activity

The Importance of Naming an Emotion

Naming an emotion gives clarity to what you're experiencing and creates distance between you and the feeling, making it easier to manage. When you put words to your emotions, your brain shifts from reacting automatically to processing more thoughtfully. This simple act helps you feel more in control, reduces emotional intensity, and allows for healthier communication and decision-making. Naming it truly helps you tame it.

HOW TO: Emotional Regulation, Name It to Tame It

1. **Pause and Breathe:** Take a few slow, deep breaths to ground yourself.
2. **Name the Emotion:** Clearly label what you're feeling (e.g., "I feel anxious," "I feel frustrated").
3. **Locate It in the Body:** Notice where in your body the emotion shows up (tight chest, tense jaw, heavy stomach, etc.).
4. **Validate the Feeling:** Remind yourself it's okay to feel this way. Say, "It makes sense, I feel this right now."
5. **Reflect on the Trigger:** Ask, "What happened that might have triggered this emotion?"
6. **Respond with Intention:** Choose a small, mindful action—like setting a boundary, asking for help, or taking a break.

Emotional Regulation Chart

What is the Emotion?	Where is it located?	What triggered me?

friday

Responding vs. Reacting

Responding vs. Reacting Through Types of Triggers: Key to Developing Emotional Awareness and Regulation

One of the most transformative skills in emotional awareness and regulation is learning the difference between reacting and responding—especially when we face emotional triggers. Triggers are situations, words, actions, or memories that provoke strong emotional reactions, often rooted in past experiences and deeply held beliefs. How we handle these moments can either keep us stuck in old patterns or open the door to healing and growth. **Reacting is typically immediate, automatic, and driven by emotion, while responding involves pause, reflection, and conscious choice.** Understanding this distinction is vital to developing emotional awareness, regulating our feelings, and exploring the underlying beliefs that influence our emotional life.

Emotional triggers often catch us off guard, activating intense feelings such as anger, fear, sadness, or shame. When we react, we typically do so impulsively, sometimes saying or doing things that later cause regret or damage relationships. For example, a comment that reminds us of past criticism may trigger a defensive outburst, even if the present situation is not as harsh. Reactivity is often fueled by unexamined beliefs, such as "I must defend myself," "I am not good enough," or "If I don't fight back, I will be hurt." These beliefs are usually formed early in life based on repeated experiences with caregivers, peers, or authority figures. Because they are deeply ingrained, triggers can cause us to revert to these automatic responses without conscious awareness.

Responding, by contrast, requires emotional awareness—the ability to recognize what we are feeling and why—and regulation, the capacity to manage our emotions and choose how to act. **When we respond, we create a moment of pause between the trigger and our action.** This pause allows us to identify the emotions the trigger has stirred up and connect them to the beliefs or past experiences that influence our reaction. For instance, if someone's tone of voice triggers feelings of abandonment rooted in childhood, responding would involve noticing this feeling, acknowledging it internally, and choosing a measured way to communicate rather than immediately withdrawing or lashing out. This thoughtful process opens the possibility for healthier interactions and emotional healing.

Understanding the types of triggers we face is crucial to improving our ability to respond rather than react. Triggers can be external, such as criticism, rejection, conflict, or perceived disrespect, or internal, such as negative self-talk, memories, or physical sensations linked to past trauma. Each type activates emotional responses tied to specific core beliefs. For example, a trigger involving rejection may activate a belief like "I am unlovable," while a trigger around failure might reflect "I am worthless unless I succeed." By identifying these connections, we gain insight into the stories that shape our emotional life and why certain situations provoke strong reactions.

Exploring these roots helps us recognize that our reactions often serve as protective mechanisms designed to keep us safe from emotional pain. While they may have been adaptive in childhood, these reactive patterns can be limiting and harmful in adult relationships and personal growth. **When we respond instead, we shift from survival mode to conscious living.** We acknowledge that while the trigger feels real and powerful, we have the capacity to choose how to engage with it. This shift is empowering and can gradually weaken the hold of old beliefs, allowing new, healthier narratives to emerge.

Developing the skill to respond rather than react requires practice and tools. Mindfulness is one such tool—it cultivates present-moment awareness and helps us notice emotional shifts as they occur. Breathing exercises, grounding techniques, and journaling can support this awareness by calming the nervous system and clarifying our internal experience. For example, pausing to take three deep breaths when feeling triggered creates a space to choose a response. Reflecting in a journal afterward can deepen understanding of the beliefs behind the trigger and how we want to move forward differently next time.

Communicating effectively is another essential part of responding. **When we respond thoughtfully, we express our emotions and needs clearly without blame or aggression.** Instead of saying, "You always make me feel worthless," a response might be, "When I hear that tone, I feel hurt and worried because of past experiences where I was criticized." This kind of communication invites empathy and connection, whereas reactive statements often escalate conflict and distance. **Responding with curiosity about both our own and others' feelings strengthens relationships and models emotional regulation.**

Over time, consistently practicing responding rather than reacting reshapes the brain and rewires emotional patterns. Neuroscience shows that pausing and labeling emotions decreases activity in the amygdala—the brain's emotional alarm center—and increases activity in the prefrontal cortex, which governs reasoning and decision-making. This means that emotional awareness and regulation are not just abstract concepts but biological processes we can strengthen through intentional practice. As a result, the power of triggers diminishes, and we experience greater emotional freedom and resilience.

In conclusion, the distinction between reacting and responding is foundational to developing emotional awareness and regulation. **Emotional triggers offer valuable information about our inner beliefs and past experiences, but how we engage with these triggers determines our growth and healing.** Reacting keeps us bound to old patterns and beliefs, often resulting in distress and damaged relationships. Responding, however, allows us to pause, reflect, and act with intention, fostering self-awareness, emotional regulation, and a deeper connection with others. By exploring the roots of our beliefs and practicing mindful responses, we move toward a more authentic, empowered, and emotionally healthy life.

Self-Assessment

Responding vs. Reacting

Instructions: Rate each statement on a scale from *1* (Strongly Disagree) to *5* (Strongly Agree).

1. When I feel triggered, I often react without thinking first.
2. I can pause and reflect before responding to emotionally intense situations.
3. My first response to conflict is usually driven by my emotions rather than reason.
4. I am able to take a breath or step back when I feel overwhelmed or provoked.
5. I later regret things I say or do when I react impulsively in emotional moments.
6. I consciously try to respond with intention rather than let my emotions take over.
7. I can recognize when I've been reactive and take steps to repair or reflect.
8. I practice tools (like grounding, breathing, or self-talk) to help me stay calm under stress.

Scoring Guide

For positively worded statements (Questions *2, 4, 6, 7, 8*): Keep the score as-is.

For negatively worded statements (Questions *1, 3, 5*): Reverse the score using this key

Original Score	Reversed Score
1	5
2	4
3	3
4	2
5	1

Total possible score: *8* (low) – *40* (high)

Range	What It Means
8–16	High Reactivity: You often respond automatically or emotionally. It's a good time to develop tools for pausing and grounding.
17–28	Growing Awareness: You're beginning to notice your reactions and are working toward more intentional responses.
29–40	Intentional Responder: You're actively practicing mindful awareness and responding thoughtfully rather than reacting impulsively.

Worksheet: Responding vs. Reacting

Instructions:

Reflect on each statement and write your thoughts in the space provided. Think about recent experiences and how you typically respond when emotionally activated or triggered.

1. When I feel triggered, I often react without thinking first. When has this happened recently? What were the results of your reaction?

    ____
    ____
    ____
    ____

2. I can pause and reflect before responding to emotionally intense situations. What helps you pause? What's one situation where you were able to respond instead of react?

    ____
    ____
    ____
    ____

3. My first response to conflict is usually driven by my emotions rather than reason.
    How do you usually feel during conflict? What thoughts or beliefs rise up quickly?

    ____
    ____
    ____
    ____

4. I am able to take a breath or step back when I feel overwhelmed or provoked. Do you have go-to grounding or calming techniques? What works best for you?

    ____
    ____
    ____
    ____

5. I later regret things I say or do when I react impulsively in emotional moments. How do you feel after a reactive moment? How do you handle those regrets?

____
____
____
____

6. I consciously try to respond with intention rather than let my emotions take over.
What helps you stay intentional? What values guide your responses?

____
____
____
____
____

7. I can recognize when I've been reactive and take steps to repair or reflect. How do you repair after a reactive moment? What supports your self-reflection?

____
____
____
____

8. I practice tools (like grounding, breathing, or self-talk) to help me stay calm under stress.
Which tools do you currently use? Which ones would you like to strengthen or try?

____
____
____
____

Reflection Questions

- What patterns did you notice in your answers?
- In what kinds of situations are you most likely to react impulsively?
- What helps you shift from reacting to responding?
- What's one small change you can make this week to respond more mindfully?

Journal

1. **Describe a time I reacted impulsively. What happened?**

2. **What could I have done differently if I had paused?**

3. **What helps me slow down before I act?**

Activity

The Importance of the STOP Method in Recognizing Emotions

The STOP method is a powerful tool for recognizing and managing emotions in the moment. It stands for **Stop, Take a breath, Observe, and Proceed.** This technique helps interrupt automatic emotional reactions, giving you a chance to pause and ground yourself. By observing what you're feeling and why, you create space for thoughtful responses instead of impulsive ones. Using the STOP method builds emotional awareness, self-regulation, and a stronger sense of control during stressful or triggering situations.

HOW TO: STOP Method

Practice using the STOP method:

S- Stop	T- Take a breath	O- Observe what's happening	P- Proceed with intention

While practicing the STOP Method, what insight did you gain?

Kathryn

Personal Recovery Story

I started using/drinking as a teenager, and was a full-blown addict by 19. I based my self-worth on others and people-pleased my way through life for years. I was very lonely in my addictions. Married and divorced multiple times, and had many boyfriends, but I felt alone. I had two children.

I hit my first treatment center at age *27* in *1984*. I also struggled with severe mental illness. I thought I had hit rock bottom in treatment, but found out it has a basement. Fast forward to *2018*, after multiple attempts in AA to get sobriety, I finally admitted to my innermost self that I was an alcoholic. I admitted this while drunk. Started going to AA again and now have 7.5 years clean and sober.

When I lost my job, my housing, my income, my relationships, and all self-respect, I had no idea that sobriety would give me back all that and more. I have a good career in the helping profession. I chair AA meetings and facilitate SMART Recovery meetings. I have good, solid relationships, and I am successful every day that I stay clean and sober. I have a new self-respect and self-confidence because I am sober. I'm able to handle some very tough stuff, like my son's suicide, one day at a time with my Higher Power. My recovery has been full of highs and lows, but it's life on life's terms, and I face it head-on.

Final Thoughts

Developing emotional awareness and regulation is a vital skill that empowers us to navigate the complexities of our inner emotional landscape with greater clarity and compassion. By learning to identify and name our emotions, we gain essential insight into what we are truly experiencing beneath the surface. This foundational awareness allows us to recognize how different types of triggers—whether external situations or internal memories—activate emotional responses tied to long-held beliefs and past experiences. Understanding these connections is crucial because it shines light on the roots of our emotional reactions, providing a pathway toward healing and transformation.

The mind-body connection plays a powerful role in this process. **Emotional triggers do not just affect our thoughts or feelings; they manifest physically in ways that can alert us to what is unfolding inside.** By tuning into bodily sensations—such as tension, racing heart, or breath changes—we can catch emotional shifts early and respond rather than react. This somatic awareness, combined with recognizing triggers, helps us build a personalized emotional regulation toolbox, filled with strategies to soothe, ground, and guide us toward healthier responses. Through this integration of mind and body, we increase resilience, reduce reactivity, and create space for mindful, intentional living.

Ultimately, the journey of exploring emotional triggers and developing regulation skills invites us to examine and challenge the core beliefs that have shaped our emotional patterns. This work deepens our self-understanding and fosters emotional freedom, allowing us to break free from old cycles and respond to life's challenges with greater ease. **As we grow in emotional intelligence and regulation, we enhance not only our relationship with ourselves but also our ability to connect authentically and empathetically with others.** This foundation creates the conditions for lasting healing, personal growth, and meaningful connection in all areas of life.

Reflection

1. **What emotions do I feel most comfortable expressing? Which ones do I tend to suppress or avoid?**

   Think about how emotions like anger, sadness, joy, or fear show up for you. Which are welcome, and which are hard to face?

   ____
   ____
   ____
   ____

2. **What helps me feel grounded, safe, and regulated when my emotions feel too big?**
   List calming tools, people, routines, or sensory experiences that support you. What else might you want to try?

   ____
   ____
   ____
   ____

3. **How can I create space to check in with myself emotionally each day?**
   Could it be a morning moment of stillness? A breath before bed? A daily journal entry? What would feel nourishing—not overwhelming?

   ____
   ____
   ____
   ____

saturday

Sober Socializing & Connection-Building

Weekend Work

Practicing healthy connection and having fun is essential in recovery because it helps rebuild trust, reduce isolation, and remind you that joy is possible without substances. Positive social experiences create a sense of belonging and support, which are key to long-term healing. Engaging in sober fun also redefines what enjoyment looks like, helping to form new habits and positive associations. Laughing, sharing experiences, and building friendships in a safe environment can strengthen your recovery foundation and boost emotional resilience.

Goal:

Practice healthy connections and have fun in safe, sober environments.

Activities:

- Game night or trivia
- Potluck and movie discussion
- Volunteer as a group at a local charity
- Community cleanup with a recovery group

10 Fun Activities I would Like to Try:
•
•
•
•
•
•
•
•
•
•

sunday

Process, Recharge, Reset, and Reflect

In seasons of recovery, healing, or transition, rest is especially vital. It offers a buffer between who we were and who we are becoming. **The space between striving and doing is where transformation is integrated.** During rest, we begin to embody the growth we've fought for—not just cognitively, but emotionally and spiritually as well.

Rest also provides a powerful opportunity to evaluate growth and lessons learned. In the quiet, we can ask ourselves reflective questions: What have I overcome? What patterns have I outgrown? What strengths have I uncovered? Without the clutter of daily noise, our growth becomes visible. We start to see how far we've come and what new values are guiding us forward.

4

Clarifying values & life purpose

Introduction

Clarifying your values and life purpose is a powerful step toward living with intention and authenticity. By identifying your core personal values—those deeply held beliefs that guide your decisions and define what truly matters—you begin to build a stronger foundation for personal growth and fulfillment. This process includes learning to distinguish between internal values (those that resonate deeply within) and external influences (like societal expectations or pressure from others), helping you reconnect with what genuinely drives and inspires you. **As you gain clarity on your life roles—such as parent, friend, worker, or community member—you begin to understand how each role contributes to your sense of purpose and overall identity.**

Once you've identified your values and purpose, the next step is to intentionally create a personal mission statement. This serves as a compass to guide your choices and actions, ensuring they are aligned with what matters most to you. **When you begin aligning your daily habits and routines with your mission and values, even small actions start to feel meaningful.** This alignment fosters a deeper sense of purpose, consistency, and empowerment in your everyday life. Living this way doesn't require perfection—it simply invites greater awareness and a commitment to showing up as your truest self.

Objective

To help individuals clarify their core values and life purpose by exploring personal beliefs, identifying internal versus external influences, and examining life roles. Participants will learn how to create a personal mission statement and align daily habits with their values to foster a greater sense of direction, authenticity, and fulfillment in everyday life.

W4: Agenda

M	Identifying Core Personal Values
T	Distinguishing Internal VS. External Influences
W	Life Roles & Purpose
T	Creating a Personal Mission Statement
F	Aligning Daily Habits
S	Reflective Growth & Planning

Monday

Identifying Core Personal Values

Identifying Core Personal Values

Foundations for Clarifying Values & Life Purpose

Our personal values are the fundamental beliefs that guide how we live, make decisions, and relate to the world around us. These values are like an internal compass that helps us navigate life's complexities, providing clarity and consistency in our choices and actions. Identifying your core personal values is a crucial step in clarifying your life purpose because values reflect what truly matters to you at your deepest level. **When you understand your values, you can align your goals, relationships, and daily behaviors in a way that supports authentic living and sustained fulfillment.**

Values develop through a lifetime of experiences, cultural influences, family teachings, and personal reflections. They are shaped by both conscious choices and subconscious programming from childhood and significant life events. For example, a person raised in a family that emphasizes honesty and integrity may carry these values strongly into adulthood, while another might prioritize creativity or independence based on different life influences. Identifying core personal values involves peeling back layers to recognize which beliefs have been inherited, which have been adopted, and which are authentically yours. This process allows you to differentiate between values imposed by external expectations and those emerging from your internal truth.

Understanding the roots of your beliefs begins with self-reflection and awareness. Many people live on autopilot, influenced unconsciously by societal norms, cultural conditioning, or peer pressure, which may not align with their genuine values. For instance, someone might pursue a high-status career because it is admired by others, rather than because it brings personal meaning or joy. **Over time, ignoring your true values can lead to dissatisfaction, internal conflict, and a sense of emptiness.** By contrast, when you clearly identify and embrace your core values, you cultivate a strong sense of purpose and integrity that sustains motivation and well-being, even in difficult times.

To begin identifying your core personal values, it helps to ask yourself several reflective questions: What principles do I refuse to compromise? When do I feel most fulfilled and authentic? What qualities do I admire in others? What activities or relationships bring me the greatest satisfaction? Writing down your answers can help clarify emerging patterns. It can also be valuable to explore moments in your life when you felt proud, deeply content, or at peace, as these often reflect alignment with your values. Conversely, consider times of frustration or regret—these may highlight situations where your actions conflicted with your true beliefs.

Another important aspect of identifying values is distinguishing between values that are truly intrinsic to you and those that are externally influenced. External influences include family expectations, cultural norms, religious teachings, or societal definitions of success. These influences are not inherently negative; they often provide meaningful structure and guidance. However, when they overshadow your internal values, they can cause dissonance and lead to choices that feel inauthentic. **Exploring the origins of your beliefs encourages you to take ownership of your values, consciously choosing which to keep, modify, or release based on your own sense of meaning.**

One effective method to clarify values is to use value lists or cards, which include words like compassion, courage, freedom, loyalty, or creativity. Reviewing such lists can help you recognize which words resonate deeply and which do not. Prioritizing your top values can further refine your understanding. Keep in mind that values are not fixed; they may evolve as you grow, learn, and experience new perspectives. The process of identifying values is ongoing, requiring openness and curiosity.

Understanding your core personal values sets the foundation for clarifying your life purpose. Life purpose is often described as the overarching reason why you do what you do—the contribution you want to make, the impact you wish to leave, or the way you want to live your days. When values and purpose align, your life feels more integrated and meaningful. For example, if one of your core values is compassion, your life purpose might involve helping others, fostering connection, or promoting justice. This alignment supports motivation, resilience, and a sense of direction even during challenges or uncertainty.

Aligning your life purpose with your values also influences your relationships, career choices, and personal goals. When you know what matters most, you can set boundaries that protect your well-being, choose work that reflects your passions, and invest in relationships that nurture your core beliefs. **Clarifying values helps you say no to opportunities that don't fit and yes to those that do, increasing satisfaction and reducing regret.**

In summary, identifying core personal values is an essential step in the journey toward living a purpose-driven life. It involves exploring the roots of your beliefs, reflecting on what matters most, and distinguishing internal values from external influences. This process fosters greater self-awareness, authenticity, and empowerment, enabling you to create a life aligned with your true self. As you continue this exploration, remember that values may shift over time, and staying connected to them requires ongoing reflection and commitment. **Ultimately, your core values serve as a beacon, guiding you toward a life of meaning, fulfillment, and integrity.**

Self-Assessment

Clarifying Values & Life Purpose

Instructions: Rate each statement on a scale from 1 (Strongly Disagree) to 5 (Strongly Agree).

1. I have a clear understanding of my core personal values.
2. I can recognize when I am being influenced by external expectations rather than my own beliefs.
3. My daily habits and routines reflect the values that matter most to me.
4. I feel a strong sense of purpose guiding my decisions and life direction.
5. I regularly reflect on my life roles and how they align with my identity and values.
6. I have written (or could easily write) a personal mission statement that represents who I am.
7. I am able to make choices that stay true to my values, even when it's difficult or unpopular.
8. I feel that my life is a true reflection of what I believe and who I want to be

Total Possible Score: *40* points (*8* questions, scored *1–5* each)

1 – Strongly Disagree	2 – Disagree	3 – Neutral /Unsure	4 – Agree	5 – Strongly Agree

Scoring Guide:

32–40 points – Strong Alignment:

You have a clear understanding of your core values and life purpose. Your daily habits, roles, and choices appear to be strongly aligned with your beliefs. You are likely living with a strong sense of authenticity and intention.

24–31 points – Moderate Alignment:

You have some awareness of your values and purpose, but there may be inconsistencies in how they show up in your daily life. This is a great time to reflect more deeply on areas that feel unclear or disconnected and explore ways to better align your habits and roles with your values.

16–23 points – Low Alignment:

You may be struggling to clearly identify your core beliefs or feel disconnected from a sense of purpose. External influences may be playing a large role in shaping your life. Consider taking time to explore your identity, values, and the influences affecting your decisions.

8–15 points – Minimal Alignment:

You may feel lost, stuck, or unsure of what truly matters to you. This is a valuable opportunity to begin the process of self-discovery. Focus on identifying core values, reflecting on your life roles, and taking small steps toward clarifying your mission and aligning your actions with your authentic self.

Journal

1. **Which values do I admire most in others, and why?**

2. **When do I feel most authentic and true to myself? What values am I honoring then?**

3. **What values do I notice guiding my biggest life decisions so far?**

Activity

The Importance of Reflecting on Values in Action

Reflecting on values in action helps you see how your core beliefs show up in your daily life, decisions, and relationships. It brings awareness to whether your actions truly align with what matters most to you—or if there's a gap that needs attention. This reflection builds integrity, deepens self-understanding, and empowers you to live with greater intention, purpose, and authenticity.

HOW TO: Values in Action Reflection

Recall 3 Peak Moments: Think of three experiences in your life that felt especially meaningful, fulfilling, or proud—moments when you felt fully alive or truly yourself.

Describe the Moment: Briefly write down what happened, who was involved, what you were doing, and how you felt.

Reflect on Why It Mattered: Ask yourself:

What about this moment was important to me?

What personal beliefs or principles were being honored?

What does this say about what I truly value?

Identify Patterns: After reflecting on all three moments, look for common themes or values that show up across them.

Values in Action Reflection

#	Peak Moment	Description	Reflection
1.			
2.			
3.			

Any Common Themes/Values That Show Up?

____

____

____

____

Tim

Personal Recovery Story

I had my first drink when I was at my uncle's wedding reception. I was 11, drank myself into a puking kid all over the dance floor. I was carried out by three people. My drinking really ramped up when I was in high school. I drank my way through high school—using every day.

When I was 18, I started at a golf organization as a Manager and a General Manager. By 21, I was taking customers, reps, etc., out. I was a drunk by the time I was 30. That is the point I lost all control. Jails, 21-day rehab, other rehab programs, and detox over 20 times. By 35, I was drinking 2-4 tall bottles a day, plus 24 or more beers. At that time, I overdosed on alcohol for the 2nd time. This time, I was brain-dead. I was in the hospital for 60 days, 30 of which I was in a coma. I had to teach myself how to walk, talk, eat, and everything else again. But, by God... I made it.

Throughout my recovery, I have utilized AA and Vivitrol (Medication Assisted Treatment). A sponsor is what helped me the most. My recovery date is July 27, 2013. Being sober, I can live life without legal trouble, yet I can still have fun. I can breathe, and I can say I am healthy.

tuesday

Distinguishing Internal vs. External Influences

Distinguishing Internal vs. External Influences

Exploring the Roots of Your Beliefs to Clarify Values & Life Purpose

Understanding the difference between internal and external influences is a fundamental step in clarifying your values and discovering your life purpose. Our beliefs, attitudes, and values are shaped by a complex interplay of factors, some arising from within ourselves, and others imposed or suggested by the outside world. Learning to distinguish between these internal and external forces is essential for authentic living because it allows you to connect with what truly matters to you—beyond social expectations, cultural norms, or pressures from others. **When you can identify which beliefs are genuinely yours and which have been adopted without reflection, you gain greater clarity, empowerment, and freedom to live purposefully.**

Internal influences refer to the ideas, feelings, motivations, and values that originate from your own experiences, intuition, conscience, and personal reflections. These are the aspects of yourself that feel deeply authentic and consistent over time. Internal influences often manifest as a strong sense of "this is right for me" or "this aligns with who I really am." They are closely linked to your sense of identity and core values. For example, you might have an internal drive toward kindness because you have experienced the value of compassion firsthand or because it resonates with your inner sense of morality. **Internal influences tend to provide lasting meaning and fulfillment because they reflect your true self.**

In contrast, external influences include the beliefs, values, and expectations communicated by family, friends, society, culture, religion, media, and institutions. These influences shape how we think and behave by setting standards for what is considered acceptable, successful, or desirable. External influences can be helpful, such as providing ethical frameworks or community belonging, but they can also be limiting when they conflict with your internal truth. For instance, you might feel pressured to pursue a certain career path because it is highly respected or financially rewarding in your culture, even if it does not resonate with your personal interests or passions. **External influences often operate subtly, making it difficult to recognize when your choices are being driven by outside forces rather than your authentic self.**

The challenge in distinguishing internal from external influences lies in the fact that many external messages become deeply ingrained over time, sometimes from early childhood. **From the moment we are born, we absorb values and beliefs from parents, teachers, peers, and the broader cultural environment.** These early influences can feel so natural that they seem like our own internal truths, even when they do not fully reflect our unique experiences or desires. For example, a person might grow up believing that success means financial wealth because it was emphasized in their family, only to later realize that their true value is creativity or freedom. Recognizing the origins of your beliefs requires intentional self-reflection and curiosity about where your thoughts and feelings come from.

One way to begin distinguishing internal and external influences is through mindful awareness and journaling. **Pay attention to moments when you feel tension, discomfort, or indecision about a choice or belief.** Ask yourself: Am I pursuing this because it feels meaningful to me, or because I think I should, according to someone else's expectations? What emotions arise when I consider following my own path? Do I feel energized and alive, or anxious and constrained? By tuning into your emotional responses, you can gain insight into whether a belief aligns with your internal values or stems from external pressure.

Another helpful approach is to examine your core values and consider how they formed. Reflect on times when you felt proud, satisfied, or authentic—what values were present in those moments? Then reflect on times when you felt conflicted or dissatisfied—did external influences play a role? Engaging in conversations with trusted others who know you well can also help, as they might observe discrepancies between your authentic self and behaviors influenced by external expectations. Sometimes, therapy or coaching provides a supportive space to explore these patterns deeply.

Distinguishing internal from external influences is especially important when clarifying your life purpose. **Life purpose is deeply tied to your internal motivations and values; it is the meaningful direction that emerges when you honor your true self.** When external influences dominate, you might find yourself living a life that looks successful on the outside but feels hollow inside. Conversely, when you align your life with your internal values, your purpose naturally unfolds, bringing a sense of fulfillment, resilience, and joy even amidst challenges.

For example, if you value connection and service internally, your life purpose might involve helping others, building relationships, or contributing to your community. However, if external messages have emphasized competition or material success, you might struggle to identify or commit to a purpose that feels satisfying. Recognizing this distinction empowers you to make conscious choices about which influences to embrace and which to question or release.

Importantly, distinguishing internal and external influences is not about rejecting all external guidance. Many external factors enrich our lives and help us grow. **The key is to evaluate these influences critically and integrate those that resonate authentically with your internal values.** This integration leads to a balanced and authentic expression of self that honors both personal truth and social connection.

The process of clarifying your values and life purpose through understanding internal versus external influences is ongoing. As you grow and experience new situations, your values may evolve, and you may need to reassess which beliefs still serve you. **Maintaining an open, curious mindset and practicing regular self-reflection can help keep you connected to your authentic path.**

In summary, distinguishing internal from external influences is a vital step in exploring the roots of your beliefs and clarifying your values and life purpose. Internal influences arise from your true self and provide lasting meaning, while external influences come from social, cultural, and relational forces that can either support or conflict with your authenticity. By increasing awareness of these forces, reflecting on your emotional and cognitive responses, and critically evaluating your beliefs, you can make empowered choices that align with your core values and guide you toward a purposeful, fulfilling life.

Self-Assessment

Distinguishing Internal vs. External Influences

Instructions: Rate each statement on a scale from *1* (Strongly Disagree) to 5 (Strongly Agree).

#	Statement	Rating
1	I often reflect on whether my decisions are guided by my own values or by other people's expectations.	
2	I can tell when I'm doing something because it feels authentic to me versus when I'm just "people-pleasing."	
3	I feel confident separating my personal beliefs from those I've inherited from family or culture.	
4	I sometimes catch myself living by values that aren't truly my own.	
5	I know the difference between what I want for my life and what others want for me.	
6	I feel pressure to conform to social or cultural norms that don't align with who I am.	
7	I make most of my important life choices based on my internal sense of what's right for me.	

#	Statement	Rating
8	I can recognize when fear of judgment is influencing my decisions more than my own truth.	

Total Score: ______ / 40

1 – Strongly Disagree	2 – Disagree	3 – Neutral /Unsure	4 – Agree	5 – Strongly Agree

Scoring Guide

32–40 points – High Self-Awareness

You are highly aware of the difference between internal and external influences. You're likely living in alignment with your true values and have strong insight into what drives your decisions.

24–31 points – Moderate Awareness

You have some awareness, but may still be influenced by external pressures without fully realizing it. It may be helpful to reflect more deeply on where your beliefs and behaviors originate.

16–23 points – Low Awareness

You may often operate on autopilot, guided more by outside expectations than your internal values. This is a good time to pause and explore the roots of your beliefs and decisions.

8–15 points – Minimal Awareness

You might be struggling to identify your own voice amid outside influences. Building self-awareness and exploring your true values can help you start aligning your life with who you really are.

Exploring Internal vs. External Influences — Visual Reflection Worksheet

Instructions:

Use this worksheet to explore and visualize the different influences that shape your beliefs and decisions. There are no right or wrong answers — just follow your intuition and creativity.

Step 1: Draw Two Circles

- On a blank sheet or the space below, draw **two large overlapping circles like a Venn diagram.** Label one circle **"Internal Influences"** and the other **"External Influences."** The area where they overlap is where internal and external influences might blend or interact.

Step 2: Fill in Each Circle

- In the **Internal Influences** circle, write or draw things that come from *within* you — your feelings, values, beliefs, experiences, instincts, and personal reflections.
- In the **External Influences** circle, write or draw things that come from *outside* of you — such as family expectations, cultural norms, social pressure, media messages, or traditions.
- In the **Overlap** section, list or illustrate influences that feel like a mix of both internal and external — beliefs or behaviors that you may have inherited but also personally accept or question.

Step 3: Reflect & Respond

- After filling the circles, take a moment to answer these questions (write or draw your responses):
- Which influences feel strongest or most familiar?
- Are there any external influences you want to explore more deeply or question?
- How do your internal influences support your authentic self?

- What can you do to honor your internal influences more fully in your daily life?

Optional Creative Extension:

- Use colors, symbols, or images that represent different influences or emotions connected to them.
- Create a small personal “shield” or “compass” drawing nearby that represents your core internal values guiding you through external pressures.

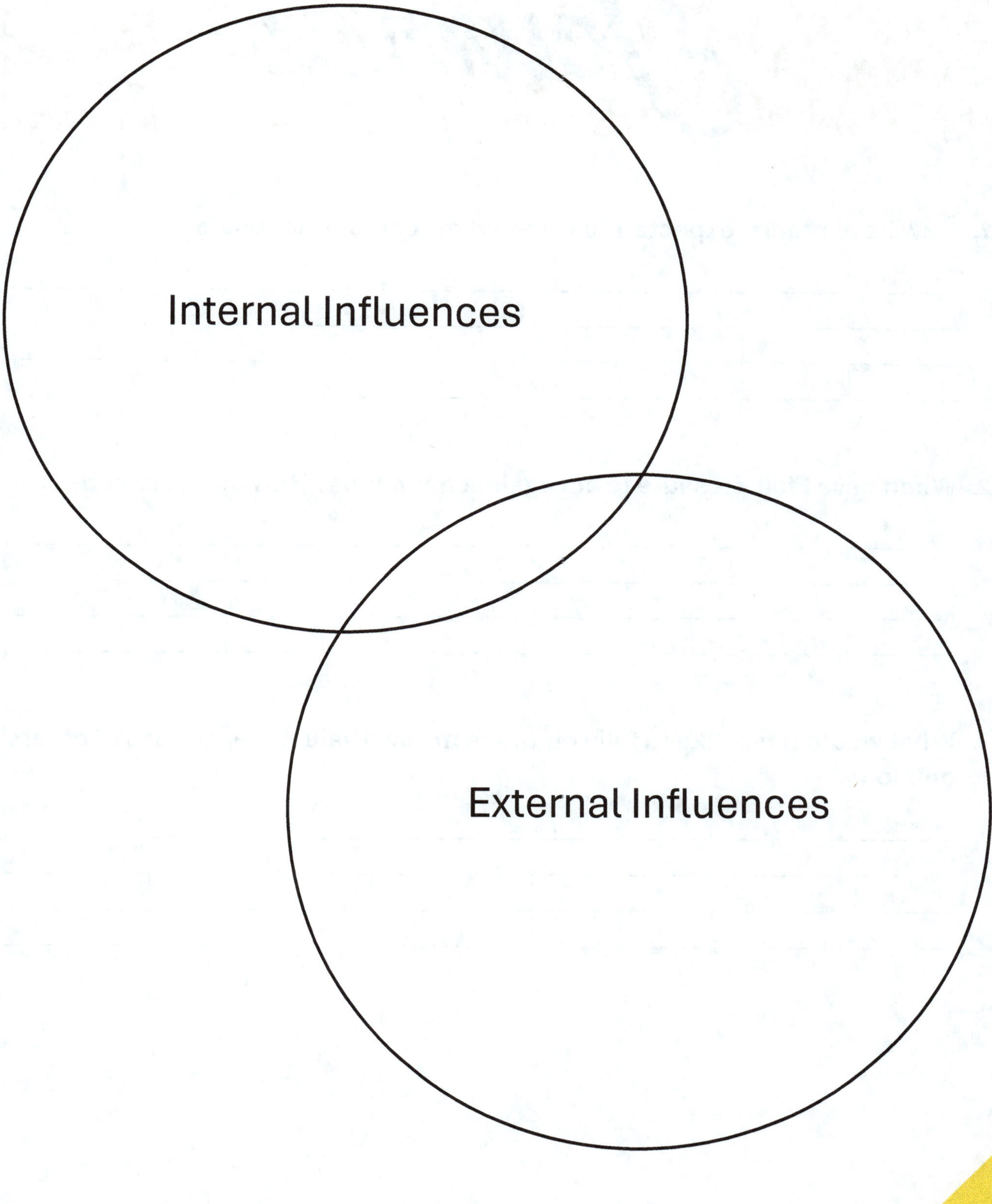
Internal Influences
External Influences

Journal

1. How have others' expectations shaped my choices or beliefs?

2. When have I felt pressure to act against my values? How did I respond?

3. What would it feel like to fully embrace my own values, regardless of others' opinions?

Activity

The Importance of Reflecting on Recent Decisions

Reflecting on recent decisions helps you understand the motivations, emotions, and thought processes behind your choices. It allows you to evaluate whether your actions align with your values, goals, and overall well-being. This kind of reflection promotes self-awareness, accountability, and growth—helping you learn from experience, celebrate progress, and make more intentional choices moving forward.

HOW TO: Reflection on Recent Decisions

Which were based on your true values?

Which were influenced by others' expectations or pressures.

Write about how it felt to follow your values vs. others' expectations.

<table>
<tr><th>Decision Based on Your True Values:</th><th>Decision Influenced by others' Expectations/ Pressures:</th></tr>
<tr><td></td><td></td></tr>
<tr><th colspan="2">REFLECTION: How does it feel to follow your values VS. Others' Expectation?</th></tr>
<tr><td></td><td></td></tr>
</table>

wednesday

Life Roles & Purpose

Life Roles & Purpose

Foundations for Clarifying Values & Life Purpose

Every individual inhabits multiple roles throughout their lifetime—such as parent, friend, employee, community member, caregiver, student, or mentor. These life roles serve as the social and personal identities through which we express ourselves and relate to others. Understanding and reflecting on your life roles is an essential step in clarifying your values and discovering your life purpose because each role carries its own set of expectations, responsibilities, and opportunities for meaning. When you become aware of these roles and how they align or conflict with your core values, you gain important insights into the roots of your beliefs and what drives your sense of fulfillment.

Life roles are often shaped by external circumstances, such as family structures, career paths, cultural traditions, and social norms. For example, becoming a parent usually comes with certain responsibilities and behaviors expected by society and family. However, how you interpret and embody that role depends greatly on your internal values and personal beliefs. One person's role as a parent might center on nurturing independence and creativity, while another might focus on safety and tradition. **Reflecting on your life roles helps you examine not only the social expectations placed upon you but also the unique ways you bring your authentic self into these roles.**

The importance of life roles in clarifying values and purpose lies in their connection to identity. We often define ourselves by the roles we play, yet this identification can sometimes mask the deeper values and beliefs that truly motivate us. For instance, someone might identify primarily as a "successful professional" and prioritize work achievements, but underneath, their core value might be connection or service to others. **By exploring your life roles, you have an opportunity to untangle the external labels and demands from your internal values.** This process helps you see where your current roles support your authentic self and where they might cause conflict or dissatisfaction.

Exploring the roots of your beliefs through life roles also encourages a more holistic understanding of your purpose. **Life purpose is not a fixed destination but an evolving sense of meaning that integrates different parts of your identity and**

experiences. Each life role offers a unique avenue to express your values and contribute to your sense of purpose. For example, in the role of a friend, your purpose might involve offering support and fostering connection, while as a worker, your purpose might be to innovate or lead with integrity. **Recognizing how your roles intersect with your values enables you to live more intentionally and create harmony between the various aspects of your life.**

Self-reflection on life roles can begin with identifying the primary roles you currently hold. Consider all the areas of your life, such as family, work, education, community involvement, hobbies, and spirituality. Writing these down can help visualize the different identities you embody. Then, reflect on how each role aligns with your core values. Which roles feel energizing and fulfilling? Which ones feel draining or misaligned? Asking yourself these questions can reveal areas where you may need to adjust your commitments, set boundaries, or reframe your understanding of a role to better fit your authentic values.

It is also helpful to consider how your life roles have evolved over time and how they might change in the future. Transitions such as becoming a parent, changing careers, or retiring can bring shifts in identity and purpose. These transitions are opportunities to reassess your values and ensure your life roles continue to reflect what matters most. Exploring past experiences where you felt a strong sense of meaning or fulfillment within a role can highlight your authentic values and offer clues about your life purpose.

Sometimes, conflicting demands from different life roles can create tension or confusion. For example, the role of a dedicated employee might feel at odds with the role of a present and nurturing parent. Clarifying your values helps you prioritize and navigate these tensions with intention. **Understanding which values are non-negotiable and which are flexible allows you to make choices that honor your whole self rather than feeling pulled in contradictory directions.** This intentional approach promotes balance and reduces feelings of guilt or overwhelm.

Moreover, consciously integrating your life roles with your personal mission or purpose statement can foster greater coherence and motivation. When your daily actions within each role reflect your core values and contribute to your purpose, you are more likely to experience satisfaction and a sense of meaning. For instance, if your value is creativity, you might seek ways to incorporate creative problem-solving in your work role or express creativity in your role as a parent through play and learning activities.

In summary, understanding and reflecting on your life roles is a vital part of clarifying your values and life purpose. Life roles provide a framework for expressing your identity, but they also come with external expectations that may or may not align with your authentic self. By exploring how each role connects to your core values and beliefs, you can uncover the roots of what motivates you and discover ways to live more intentionally. **This process not only supports personal fulfillment but also empowers you to navigate life transitions and conflicting demands with greater clarity and confidence.** Ultimately, aligning your life roles with your values and purpose enriches your sense of meaning and helps you live a more integrated and authentic life.

Self-Assessment

Life Roles & Purpose

Instructions: Rate each statement on a scale from *1* (Strongly Disagree) to *5* (Strongly Agree).

#	Statement	Rating
1	I have identified the major roles I play in my life (e.g., parent, friend, worker) and understand their importance.	
2	I feel that my different life roles align well with my core values.	
3	I experience a sense of purpose through at least one of my life roles.	
4	I regularly reflect on how my life roles influence my sense of identity.	
5	I feel fulfilled and satisfied in the way I live out my life roles.	
6	When life roles conflict, I can navigate the tension in a way that honors my values and priorities.	
7	I see how my life roles contribute to my overall life purpose.	
8	I intentionally choose how I spend my time and energy across my different roles to support my purpose.	

Total Score: ______ / 4

1 – Strongly Disagree	2 – Disagree	3 – Neutral /Unsure	4 – Agree	5 – Strongly Agree

Scoring Guide

- **32–40 points – Strong Role-Purpose Alignment**

You have a clear understanding of your life roles and how they connect to your purpose. You likely experience fulfillment and coherence in your identity.

- **24–31 points – Moderate Alignment**

You have some awareness of your roles and purpose, but may notice occasional misalignment or confusion. Reflection and intentional adjustments can strengthen this connection.

- **16–23 points – Low Alignment**

You might feel disconnected from some life roles or uncertain about how they fit with your purpose. Exploring your values and role expectations can help create balance.

- **8–15 points – Minimal Alignment**

You may struggle to find meaning in your roles or feel conflicted by competing demands. This is a good opportunity for deep reflection and redefining your life purpose.

Life Roles & Purpose Reflection — Visual Activity

Instructions:

Use this worksheet to explore your life roles and how they connect to your sense of purpose. There is no right or wrong way—draw, write, or doodle what feels right to you.

Step 1: Draw Your Life Roles

Draw a large circle in the center of the page and label it **"Me / My Core Self."** Around this circle, draw several smaller circles (or bubbles) radiating outward. Each smaller circle represents an important **life role** you play (e.g., parent, friend, employee, student, caregiver, artist).

Step 2: Add Descriptions & Feelings

Inside or near each life role circle, write or draw:

- What this role means to you
- How does this role make you feel (energized, stressed, fulfilled, conflicted, etc)
- How do you believe this role connects to your values or purpose

Use colors, symbols, or words to express your feelings about each role.

Step 3: Reflect on Alignment

Look at your drawing and answer (write or doodle your thoughts):

- Which roles feel most aligned with your core self?
- Are there roles that feel disconnected or draining? Why?
- How do these roles support or challenge your life purpose?
- What role would you like to invest more energy in?
- Are there any roles you want to change, release, or redefine?

Optional Creative Extension:

- Draw arrows showing how your roles interact or conflict.
- Create a symbol or image representing your overall life purpose in the center circle.
- Use different colors or shapes to highlight the roles you want to focus on or shift.

This visual exercise helps you deepen awareness of your identity and purpose, highlighting where your life roles nourish or challenge you.

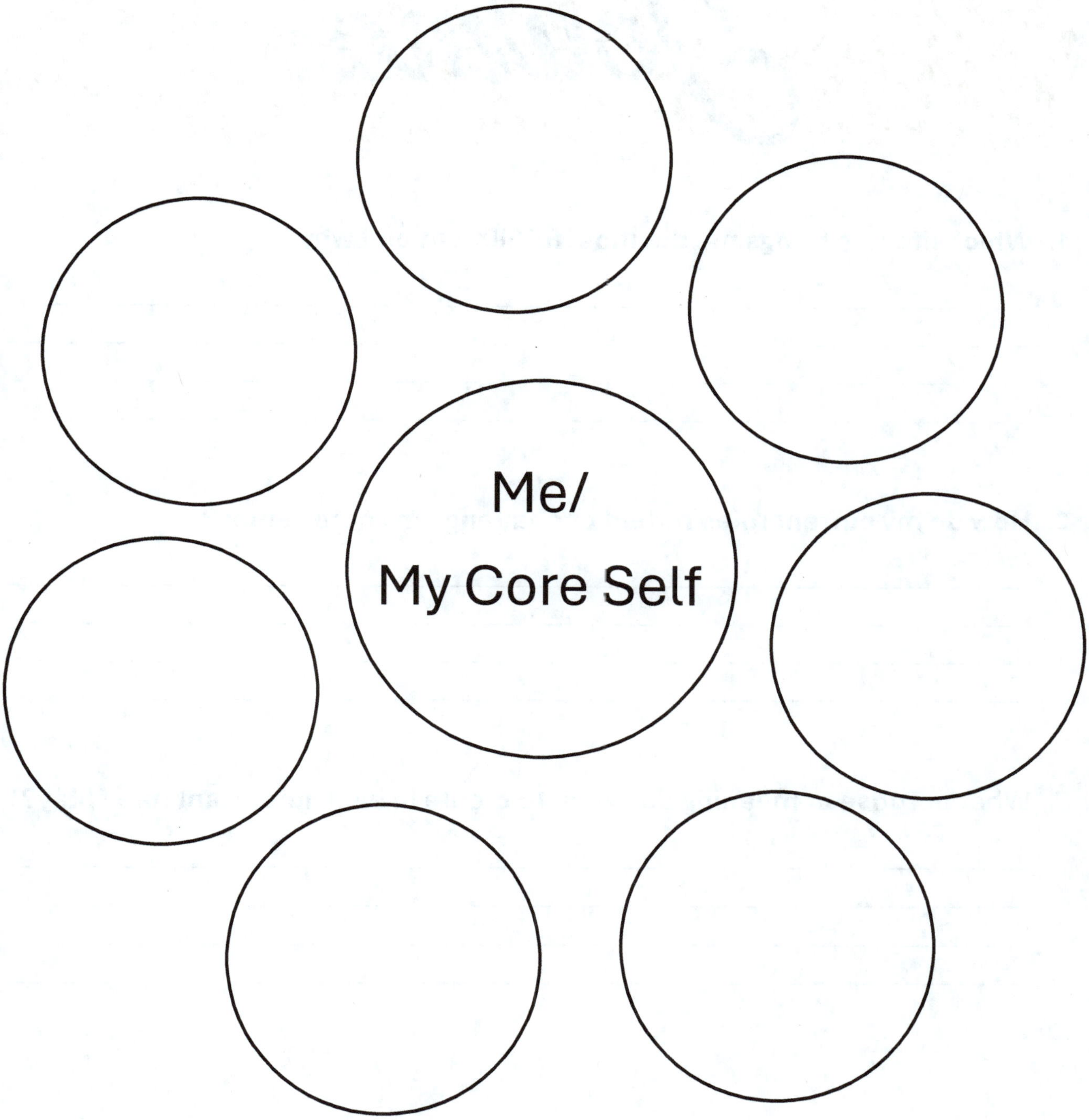
Me/
My Core Self

Journal

1. Which life role brings me the most fulfillment and why?

2. How do my current roles reflect or challenge my core values?

3. What purpose or meaning do I want to create in each important role I play?

Activity

The Importance of Recognizing Your Current Life Role

Recognizing your current life role—such as caregiver, student, worker, or friend—helps you understand how your identity, responsibilities, and energy are being shaped in the present moment. It brings awareness to how this role impacts your priorities, emotions, and personal growth. By acknowledging where you are now, you can better assess whether this role aligns with your values and goals, and decide how you want to show up or evolve in this season of life.

HOW TO: List Your Current Life Roles

(family member, worker, friend, student, etc.).

For each role, answer:

- What is meaningful to me in this role?
- How does this role align with my values?
- How can I bring more purpose to this role?

My Current Life Roles

Current Life Role	Why is this role meaningful?	Does this role align with my values?	How Can I Bring More Purpose?

thursday

Creating a Personal Mission Statement

Creating a Personal Mission Statement

A Pathway to Clarifying Values & Life Purpose

A personal mission statement is a powerful tool that encapsulates your core values, beliefs, and life purpose into a clear, guiding declaration. It serves as a compass, helping you navigate decisions, challenges, and opportunities with intentionality and clarity. Creating a personal mission statement is a vital step in the process of clarifying your values and life purpose because it distills your deepest motivations into words that inspire and direct your everyday actions. **By articulating what truly matters to you, a mission statement supports greater self-awareness, alignment, and fulfillment.**

The roots of your personal mission statement lie in your core values and beliefs. These are the foundational elements that shape how you view yourself, your relationships, and your contributions to the world. Often, these values develop through a combination of personal experiences, cultural background, family influences, and internal reflections. Exploring the origins of your beliefs—why certain principles resonate with you or how past experiences have shaped your worldview—deepens the authenticity of your mission statement. This exploration invites you to move beyond external expectations or societal pressures and connect with what truly drives you from within.

Creating a personal mission statement begins with self-reflection and honesty. It requires asking yourself profound questions, such as: What do I stand for? What kind of person do I want to be? What impact do I wish to have on others and the world? What values guide my choices and behavior? What are my unique strengths and passions? By thoughtfully considering these questions, you can uncover themes and ideas that form the backbone of your mission. **Writing down your answers without censorship helps surface your authentic voice and priorities.**

One useful approach is to review lists of common values—such as integrity, compassion, creativity, growth, or service—and identify which resonate most deeply with you. This process helps clarify your core principles and filters out less relevant influences. **It is important to be patient and open during this exploration because values may shift or become clearer over time.** The goal is to create a mission statement that feels meaningful and true to who you are, not one that sounds impressive or meets external expectations.

Once you have identified your core values and reflected on your purpose, you can begin drafting your mission statement. Unlike a generic life goal, a personal mission statement is broader and more enduring—it expresses your fundamental reason for being and how you want to live your life consistently. Effective mission statements are usually concise, inspirational, and written in the present tense. For example, a mission statement might be: "To live with integrity and compassion, fostering growth and connection in myself and others," or "To use creativity and empathy to inspire positive change in my community." These statements guide behavior and provide a reference point when faced with decisions or challenges.

The importance of a personal mission statement lies in its ability to bring coherence and focus to your life. **When your daily actions and long-term goals align with your mission, you experience greater motivation, resilience, and satisfaction.** Your mission acts as a filter for opportunities, helping you decide which to pursue and which to decline based on whether they support your deeper purpose. **In moments of uncertainty or difficulty, your mission can serve as a grounding reminder of what matters most, helping you stay true to yourself.**

Moreover, a personal mission statement fosters intentionality in relationships and personal growth. By clearly defining your values and purpose, you can communicate more authentically with others, build connections based on shared principles, and set boundaries that protect your well-being. It also supports ongoing self-reflection and adaptation; as you evolve, your mission statement can be revisited and refined to reflect new insights or life stages. **This dynamic quality makes the mission statement a living document rather than a static statement.**

Exploring the roots of your beliefs during the mission statement creation process is particularly valuable because it encourages self-awareness and integration. **Understanding why certain values are meaningful can reveal underlying needs, desires, or wounds that shape your worldview.** For instance, valuing honesty deeply might stem from past experiences where trust was broken. Recognizing these connections allows you to approach your mission with compassion and depth, fostering healing and growth alongside clarity.

In practical terms, creating a personal mission statement can be done in stages. Start with freewriting or journaling about your values, passions, and goals. Then, identify recurring themes and craft several draft statements. Test these drafts by imagining how they would guide you in specific situations or decisions. Seek feedback from trusted friends, mentors, or coaches to gain perspective. Finally, refine your statement into a concise, affirmative declaration that feels inspiring and authentic.

In summary, creating a personal mission statement is a transformative practice that helps clarify your values and life purpose by articulating the roots of your beliefs into a meaningful guide. It enhances self-awareness, supports intentional living, and provides a stable foundation for navigating life's complexities. By investing time and reflection into this process, you cultivate a sense of direction and alignment that enriches your personal and interpersonal experiences. **Your mission statement becomes a beacon that lights your path, encouraging you to live with purpose, integrity, and passion every day.**

Self-Assessment

Creating a Personal Mission Statement

Instructions: Rate each statement on a scale from *1* (Strongly Disagree) to *5* (Strongly Agree).

#	Statement	Rating
1	I have a clear and written personal mission statement that reflects my core values and purpose.	
2	My mission statement helps guide my decisions and daily actions.	
3	I feel inspired and motivated by my personal mission statement.	
4	I regularly revisit and reflect on my mission statement to ensure it aligns with who I am becoming.	
5	Writing a mission statement helped me understand the roots of my beliefs and values.	
6	My mission statement feels authentic and true to my inner self.	
7	When faced with difficult choices, I use my mission statement to help me decide what is right for me.	
8	My personal mission statement supports me in living intentionally and with purpose.	

Total Score: ______ / 40

1 – Strongly Disagree	2 – Disagree	3 – Neutral /Unsure	4 – Agree	5 – Strongly Agree

Scoring Guide

32–40 points – Strong Connection:

You have a well-defined and meaningful personal mission statement that effectively guides your life and decisions.

24–31 points – Moderate Connection:

You have a mission statement or sense of purpose, but there may be opportunities to clarify or deepen its impact.

16–23 points – Developing Connection:

You may be in the early stages of creating a mission statement or understanding your purpose. More reflection and refinement could be helpful.

8–15 points – Minimal Connection:

You might not have a clear mission statement yet or find it difficult to connect with your purpose. Starting the process could provide greater clarity and direction.

Values & Beliefs Discovery Worksheet for Your Personal Mission Statement

Instructions:

Take your time to reflect on each section. There are no right or wrong answers. This is about discovering what truly matters to you and understanding the roots of your beliefs.

Step 1: Identify Your Core Values

Below are some common values. Circle the ones that resonate deeply with you. Add any others that are important but not listed.

Examples of Core Values:

Integrity | Compassion | Growth | Creativity | Honesty | Courage | Connection | Service | Respect | Freedom | Learning | Family | Justice | Balance | Gratitude | Responsibility | Faith | Innovation | Patience | Kindness

Your Core Values (circle or add):

____

____

____

____

Step 2: Reflect on What These Values Mean to You

Choose 3–5 of the values you circled or added. For each, write a few sentences about why it matters to you and how it shows up in your life.

Value: ____________________

Why it matters to me:

____

____

How I express this value:

Value: ____________________

Why it matters to me:

How I express this value:

Value: ____________________

Why it matters to me:

How I express this value:

Step 3: Explore the Roots of Your Beliefs

Think about where these values came from. Answer these questions honestly:

- Did I learn these values from family, culture, personal experience, or something else?
- Are these values truly mine, or do I feel pressure to adopt them?
- How have my experiences shaped my beliefs about what's important?

Write your thoughts here:

____

____

____

____

Step 4: Draft Your Personal Mission Statement Ideas

Using your core values and reflections, try writing 1–3 sentences that describe:

- Who you want to be
- What do you want to contribute to or stand for
- How do you want to live your life

Examples:

- *"To live with integrity and kindness, fostering connection and growth in myself and others."*
- "To use creativity and courage to make a positive impact in my community."

Your draft(s):

____

____

____

____

Step 5: Reflection Questions

- How does this mission statement feel? Authentic? Inspiring? Clear?

- What parts of your values or beliefs does it capture well?
- What might you want to add or change?

Write your thoughts:

____

____

____

____

Journal

1. **What three words describe the person I aspire to be?**

2. **What impact do I want to have on the people around me or the world?**

3. **How can I express my values through a clear mission statement?**

Activity

The Importance of Recognizing Your Personal Mission

Recognizing your personal mission and putting it into words helps you clarify your purpose, values, and the direction you want your life to take. Writing a mission statement acts as a compass, guiding your decisions, goals, and actions with intention and meaning. It grounds you in who you are and what matters most, especially during times of transition, challenge, or growth.

HOW TO: Write a Personal Mission Statement

Using your values and reflections, write a personal mission statement. This can be one or two sentences describing the kind of person you want to be and what you want to contribute to life.

My Values & Beliefs

My Personal Mission Statement

friday

Aligning Daily Habits

Aligning Daily Habits: Connecting Actions to Core Beliefs & Identity

Daily habits are the small, often automatic behaviors that shape much of our lives. Though they may seem insignificant on their own, over time, these habits accumulate and form patterns that directly reflect and reinforce our core beliefs and identity. **Aligning daily habits with your core beliefs is essential for living authentically and intentionally.** When your habits support the values and truths you hold deep inside, you create a foundation for meaningful growth and a coherent sense of self. Conversely, habits that conflict with your beliefs can generate internal tension, confusion, and dissatisfaction.

Core beliefs are the fundamental assumptions you hold about yourself, others, and the world. They develop from early experiences, cultural context, and ongoing reflections, shaping your identity and worldview. For example, a core belief might be "I am worthy of love" or "The world is a safe place." These beliefs influence how you perceive situations, make decisions, and respond emotionally. Because habits are the concrete expressions of these beliefs, examining your daily routines offers valuable insights into your identity's roots. By becoming aware of whether your habits align or clash with your core beliefs, you can better understand yourself and identify areas for transformation.

The importance of aligning habits with core beliefs and identity lies in the way habits reinforce neural pathways and behavioral patterns. **When your daily actions are consistent with your values, you strengthen positive self-concepts and promote psychological well-being.** For example, if one of your core beliefs is that health and self-care are important, adopting habits such as regular exercise, balanced eating, and sufficient rest support that belief, enhancing your sense of integrity and self-respect. On the other hand, if your habits involve neglecting self-care despite valuing it internally, you may experience cognitive dissonance—a psychological discomfort that arises when behaviors contradict beliefs. This dissonance can lead to stress, reduced motivation, and a fragmented sense of identity.

Aligning daily habits begins with self-awareness and honest reflection. Many habits operate on autopilot, embedded in routines that may have been established years ago or influenced by environmental cues rather than conscious choice. Taking stock of your current habits—both helpful and unhelpful—allows you to see where your behaviors support or undermine your core beliefs. This process might involve journaling about your daily routines, noting which actions feel authentic and which feel forced or out of sync. Mindfulness practices can also enhance awareness by helping you observe your behaviors without judgment and identify patterns that may have been invisible before.

Once you have identified habits that do not align with your core beliefs, the next step is intentional change. Changing habits can be challenging because it requires disrupting automatic patterns and building new neural pathways. However, when the motivation is grounded in your authentic values and identity, change becomes more sustainable and meaningful. For example, if you deeply value connection but notice that habitual social withdrawal conflicts with this, you can intentionally create small habits that foster relationships, such as regular check-ins with friends or participating in community activities. These aligned habits gradually reinforce your value of connection and shift your self-perception.

It is also helpful to approach habit alignment with compassion and patience. **Change rarely occurs overnight, and setbacks are a natural part of growth.** Viewing habits as experiments rather than pass/fail tests encourages a growth mindset. Celebrating small successes helps build momentum and reinforces your commitment to living in accordance with your core beliefs. Additionally, surrounding yourself with supportive environments and relationships can make habit change easier by providing encouragement and accountability.

Aligning daily habits with your core beliefs also strengthens your sense of identity by creating consistency between your internal world and external actions. Identity is not static but a dynamic interplay between who you believe yourself to be and how you express yourself in the world. **When your habits embody your core values, you experience greater coherence and authenticity.** For instance, if you identify as a compassionate person, habitual acts of kindness and empathy reinforce that identity. This consistency enhances self-esteem and fosters resilience, enabling you to navigate challenges without losing sight of your true self.

Furthermore, examining and aligning habits offers an opportunity to explore the roots of your beliefs more deeply. Some habits may have been shaped by childhood experiences, cultural conditioning, or trauma and may no longer serve your current values or goals. By bringing conscious awareness to these patterns, you can begin to question inherited or outdated beliefs and choose new ways of being that reflect your evolving identity. This process of reflection and adjustment supports personal growth and empowerment.

In practical terms, aligning daily habits might involve creating a clear plan that connects specific actions to your core beliefs. Setting achievable goals, breaking larger changes into manageable steps, and using reminders or habit trackers can support this process. **Regularly revisiting your values and mission statement helps maintain focus and motivation.** For example, if a core belief is environmental stewardship, aligning habits might include reducing waste, conserving energy, or supporting sustainable products—concrete actions that bring your values to life.

In summary, aligning daily habits with your core beliefs and identity is a foundational practice for authentic living and personal growth. Habits are the bridge between your internal values and your external life, shaping how you experience yourself and the world. By increasing awareness of your habits, reflecting on their origins, and intentionally adjusting them to reflect your true beliefs, you create coherence, integrity, and meaning. This alignment not only enhances well-being but also fosters resilience and confidence, empowering you to live a life that is true to who you are at the deepest level.

Self-Assessment

Aligning Daily Habits with Core Values

Instructions: Rate each statement on a scale from 1 (Strongly Disagree) to 5 (Strongly Agree).

#	Statement	Rating
1	My daily habits reflect the values that are most important to me.	
2	I feel that my routines support my overall well-being and life goals.	
3	When I notice a habit that doesn't align with my values, I take steps to change it.	
4	I am intentional about how I spend my time each day to honor my core beliefs.	
5	I feel authentic and true to myself in my everyday actions.	
6	I regularly reflect on whether my habits are helping me grow in the direction I want.	
7	I experience less internal conflict because my behaviors match my values.	
8	I find it easier to make decisions when I keep my core values in mind.	

Total Score: ______ / 40

1 – Strongly Disagree	2 – Disagree	3 – Neutral /Unsure	4 – Agree	5 – Strongly Agree

Scoring Guide

- **32–40 points – Strong Alignment**

Your daily habits closely reflect your core values, supporting a consistent and authentic life.

- **24–31 points – Moderate Alignment**

You are somewhat aware of the connection between habits and values, but could benefit from deeper intentionality.

- **16–23 points – Low Alignment**

There may be frequent gaps between your habits and values. Exploring and adjusting habits can increase your alignment.

- **8–15 points – Minimal Alignment**

Your habits often conflict with your values. Reflecting on and changing daily routines could greatly improve your sense of authenticity and well-being.

Aligning Daily Habits with Core Values

Reflect & Plan Worksheet

Step 1: Identify Your Core Values

List 3–5 values that are most important to you (e.g., honesty, kindness, growth, balance):

____

____

____

____

Step 2: Reflect on Your Current Habits

Write down some daily habits or routines you currently have:

____

____

____

____

Step 3: Explore Alignment

For each habit, note whether it supports or conflicts with your values, and why:

Habit Supports or Conflicts? How does it relate to your values?

____

____

____

____

Step 4: Plan Small Changes

Choose 1–3 habits to adjust or develop that better align with your core values. Write what you will do and how:

	Habit to Change or Add	How I Will Change or Develop It	Why It Matters (Connection to Value)
1.			
2.			
3.			

Step 5: Intentions for Daily Living

Write a short intention or affirmation that reflects your commitment to living your values through your daily habits:

Example:
"I choose to act with kindness and integrity in all my daily interactions."

Your intention:

____

____

____

____

Self-Assessment

1. **Which daily habits support my values and bring me closer to my purpose?**

2. **What habits or routines do I want to change because they don't align with my mission?**

3. **What is one small action I can take today to live more intentionally according to my values?**

Activity

Aligning Daily Habits

Aligning daily habits with your core values and goals is essential because it turns your everyday actions into meaningful steps toward the life you want. When your habits reflect what truly matters to you, you feel more motivated, focused, and fulfilled. This alignment helps reduce wasted time and energy on activities that don't serve you, making personal growth and positive change more natural and sustainable.

HOW TO: Habit Alignment

1. Write down three important things you care about (values or goals).
2. List five habits you do every day.
3. Next to each habit, ask yourself:
    - *Does this habit help me with what I care about? Yes or No*
4. Pick one habit that doesn't help and think:
    - *What small change can I make to better support what I care about?*
5. Write a short sentence about how you want to change your habits to match your goals.

3 Important Things I Care About:

____

____

____

____

5 Daily Habits I Do Every Day:

Daily Habit	Does this Habit Help Me with What I Care About?

Which Habit DOES NOT Help.

Reflect on how you want to change your habits to match your goals.

Jeffry

Personal Recovery Story

My name is Jeffry. I was 2 months premature. My mother was told I would not live long at all, and there was nothing they could do. My mother took me home to die (supposedly) in her arms. So, I was a weaker child. At 8, I was struck by an automobile. Several doctors from 4 states said there was no chance of my surviving, so they scheduled to turn me off. While three floors of the hospital were flooded with several churches praying for me, I woke up telling a story of walking with Jesus and being given a choice to stay with my mother.

Doctors gave strict instructions regarding my limitations for the rest of my life. God had other plans. So in my mid-teens, finally being like most young men, I still felt out of place—something was missing. I thrived in construction; crane and rigging is my thing. After 30 years of liquor, cocaine, and women, I hit ROCK BOTTOM. Lost everything. Walked into a recovery center with only the clothes on my back, breath in my lungs, and God's Grace and Mercy. I worked the 12 steps of Alcoholics Anonymous to the hilt. I met my sponsor on day 3, jumped into his ministry and church 8 hours a week. 06/28/2025 makes two complete years completely sober.

God granted me my career back and has answered many prayers 10-fold. I continue to help pull as many men as possible from that same pit I was once in. Few people use only AA to get sober. How sad they miss such an EXTRAORDINARY OPPORTUNITY to grow a relationship with God. This life is short, and if we don't keep short accounts with God all day, we will miss His directions to exit exile, detour hell, and come back home—heaven-bound. Thank you for reading, and I hope it helped plant a seed. All Glory to God.

Final Thoughts

Clarifying your core values and life purpose is a transformative journey of self-discovery that invites you to explore the roots of your beliefs and what truly matters to you. Understanding the difference between internal influences—those deeply held, authentic beliefs—and external pressures or societal expectations empowers you to reclaim your voice and live with greater integrity. Reflecting on your various life roles helps you see how your identity is expressed and shaped by both your values and the expectations placed upon you, offering insight into areas where your life is in alignment or needs adjustment.

Creating a personal mission statement is a powerful way to distill your core values and purpose into a guiding declaration that inspires intentional living. It serves as a compass, helping you make decisions and set goals that resonate with your authentic self. **When your mission aligns with your daily habits, your actions become expressions of your true identity, fostering consistency, meaning, and fulfillment.** This alignment reduces inner conflict and supports ongoing growth by reinforcing the connection between what you believe and how you live.

Ultimately, the process of clarifying values, distinguishing influences, exploring life roles, crafting a mission statement, and aligning habits is an ongoing practice that cultivates self-awareness, authenticity, and purpose. It invites you to live deliberately rather than on autopilot, empowering you to navigate life's complexities with confidence and clarity. **By continually exploring and honoring your core beliefs, you create a foundation for a life that feels meaningful, coherent, and deeply your own.**

Reflection

1. **What really matters to me, beyond what I've been taught, should matter?** Name the values, people, dreams, or causes that light you up. What do you care about deeply?

2. **If I lived a life fully aligned with my values, what would change?** What would you say "yes" to more often? What would you say "no" to without guilt?

3. **If I could write a letter to my future self 5 years from now, what would I hope for them to know, feel, or remember?** Let your future vision speak with warmth and hope. You don't have to know all the "how" yet—just the "why."

saturday

Reflection Growth & Planning

Weekend Work

Creating space for self-reflection, goal-setting, and intention-building is vital in recovery as it helps you pause, evaluate your progress, and stay aligned with your values. It allows you to make sense of where you've been, where you are now, and where you want to go. This intentional time fosters clarity, accountability, and motivation, helping you set meaningful goals that support your healing. **By regularly checking in with yourself, you strengthen your sense of purpose and create a roadmap for continued growth and transformation.**

Goal:

Create space for self-reflection, goal-setting, and intention-building.

Activities:

- Weekend check-in & goal review session
- Guided meditation and gratitude journaling
- Recovery step study or discussion group
- Personal values or life purpose workshop

10 Goal-Setting Activities I would Like to Try:
•
•
•
•
•
•
•
•
•
•

sunday

To Process, Recharge, Reset, and Reflect

The Importance of Rest: To Process, Recharge, Reset, and Reflect- Part 4

Rest invites planning and potential pivoting. With a clearer head and a regulated nervous system, we can think more strategically. Are we still aligned with our goals? Is there something new calling us? Do we need to make a shift, set a boundary, or try a different path? Rest opens the door to intentional living rather than reactive survival.

Ultimately, rest is not a luxury—it's a necessity. It is the fertile soil where resilience is strengthened, insight blooms, and purpose is reawakened. By giving ourselves permission to pause, we gain far more than we lose. We return with sharper clarity, deeper peace, and a renewed vision for the journey ahead.

BONUS!!

Activity

Letter to Your Future Self

Instructions:

Take a moment to reflect on the past 30 days and write a letter to yourself as if you are speaking from today to a future version of yourself — perhaps one month, three months, or even a year from now. Be honest, encouraging, and loving. This letter is a tool to remind yourself of your growth, your values, and your commitment to living authentically.

Guiding Prompts:

1. **Acknowledge Your Growth:**
    - What have you learned about yourself during this 30-day journey?
    - What challenges did you face, and how did you overcome them?
2. **Celebrate Your Strengths:**
    - Which qualities, skills, or insights are you proud of?
    - How have your habits, emotional awareness, or sense of purpose strengthened?
3. **Affirm Your Values & Purpose:**
    - Which core values do you want to continue honoring?
    - What intentions do you have for living a life aligned with your purpose?
4. **Encourage Your Future Self:**
    - What reminders or advice would you give your future self to stay on track?
    - How can you continue practicing self-awareness, emotional regulation, and intentional living?

Letter Template:

Dear Future Me,

I want to remind you of the growth and courage you have shown over the past 30 days. You took the time to explore your core beliefs, understand your triggers, and develop emotional awareness. You faced challenges with honesty and compassion, and you celebrated even the small steps forward.

Remember the values that matter most to you: ______________________________ (fill in your core values). Let them guide your decisions, your habits, and the way you show up in your life every day. Stay connected to your purpose and continue aligning your actions with the person you are becoming.

When challenges arise, remember that you are resilient, capable, and worthy of living authentically. Keep practicing self-awareness, honoring your emotions, and making choices that reflect your true self. Celebrate your progress, no matter how small, and continue moving forward with courage and intention.

I believe in you, and I know that you can continue creating a life of meaning, joy, and alignment with your values. Keep showing up for yourself, trusting your journey, and honoring the growth you've achieved.

With love and encouragement,

Yourself

30-Day Program Wrap-Up: Stepping Into Your True Self

Congratulations on completing this 30-day journey! Over the past month, you have invested time and energy into exploring who you are, what you believe, and how you want to live. This work is not just about learning new information — it's about transformation, growth, and creating a deeper connection with yourself.

Throughout this program, you began by **exploring your core beliefs and identity,** uncovering the roots of what drives your thoughts, behaviors, and decisions. You identified the stories you've carried, and you had the courage to question which ones still serve you and which ones you are ready to release. This awareness is the foundation of lasting change — understanding *who you are* and giving yourself permission to honor that truth.

You also spent time **understanding your triggers and patterns,** recognizing the moments that spark emotional reactions and the cycles you may have repeated without even realizing it. By naming and noticing these triggers, you built the ability to pause, reflect, and respond in healthier ways — rather than being stuck in old habits. This is how healing begins: with compassion, curiosity, and conscious choice.

Building on that, you learned tools for **developing emotional awareness and regulation,** tuning into your feelings instead of pushing them away or letting them take over. You practiced noticing your emotions, naming them, and choosing how to respond in ways that align with your best self. This skill will serve you in every area of life — in relationships, work, and personal well-being.

Finally, you focused on **clarifying your values and life purpose,** reflecting on what matters most and how you want to show up in the world. You've started the process of aligning your habits, roles, and decisions with your true values so that your daily life reflects the person you are becoming.

As you move forward beyond this 30-day program, remember that growth is a lifelong process. **The work you've done here is a starting point, not an ending.** Keep reflecting on your core beliefs, practicing emotional regulation, and realigning with your values whenever life feels off course. Every step you take — even the smallest ones — moves you closer to a life of authenticity, purpose, and peace.

You are capable. You are resilient. And you are worthy of living a life that reflects your true self. **Keep showing up for yourself, stay curious about your journey, and celebrate the progress you've made.** The next chapter of your life is yours to write — and you now have the tools to write it with intention and courage.

If this book resonated with you and supported your journey toward growth and healing, I invite you to explore Melissa McKinney's other books; one is out now, and many more are to follow!

Told through a series of journal-style reflections, **LESSONS LEARNED** is a deeply personal, darkly humorous, and profoundly inspiring account of a woman who fought her way back from chaos to clarity. With biting wit and fearless vulnerability, Melissa lays bare the struggles, triumphs, and everyday realities of navigating life without the crutches of addiction. From the sobering firsts-first holiday sober, first Friday night without a drink-to the unexpected lessons in self-worth, relationships, and learning to say "no," this book is a testament to resilience and the power of transformation. More than just a recovery story, **LESSONS LEARNED** is a rallying cry for anyone who has ever felt lost, trapped, or unsure of who they are. It's a reminder that even in the messiest of pasts, there is hope, humor, and an undeniable strength waiting to be uncovered. This is not just a book about quitting drinking. It's a book about finally starting to live.

www.ingramcontent.com/pod-product-compliance
Lightning Source LLC
LaVergne TN
LVHW080031210926
848481LV00011B/3156